PUT YOUR DREAM
TO THE TEST

PUT YOUR DREAM TO THE TEST

10 Questions That Will Help
You See It and Seize It

JOHN C. MAXWELL

THOMAS NELSON
Since 1798

NASHVILLE   DALLAS   MEXICO CITY   RIO DE JANEIRO   BEIJING

Published in Nashville, Tennessee, by Thomas Nelson. Thomas Nelson is a registered trademark of Thomas Nelson, Inc.

Published in association with Yates & Yates, www.yates2.com.

Page design by Mandi Cofer.

Thomas Nelson, Inc., titles may be purchased in bulk for educational, business, fund-raising, or sales promotional use. For information, please e-mail Special Markets@ThomasNelson.com.

Scripture quotations taken from *The Living Bible*, © 1971. Used by permission of Tyndale House Publishers, Inc., Wheaton, Illinois 60189. All rights reserved.

ISBN 978-1-4002-8066-7 (IE)

Library of Congress Cataloging-in-Publication Data
Maxwell, John C., 1947–
  Put your dream to the test : 10 questions that will help you see it and seize it / John C. Maxwell.
    p. cm.
  Includes bibliographical references.
  ISBN 978-0-7852-1412-0
  1. Success in business. 2. Success. 3. Conduct of life. I. Title.
  HF5386.M4447 2008
  650.1--dc22

2008044839

Printed in the United States of America
09 10 11 12 13 RRD 7 6 5 4 3 2

This book is dedicated to Margaret Maxwell,
the girl of my dreams. On June 14, 1969, we were married.
Since that day, we have been living the dream together.
I cannot imagine my life without her. Margaret, happy 60/40!

CONTENTS

Contents

ACKNOWLEDGMENTS

Thank you to
Charlie Wetzel, my writer
Stephanie Wetzel, who proofed and edited the manuscript
Sue Caldwell, who typed the first draft
Linda Eggers, my assistant

What Is Your Dream?

What is your dream? Will you achieve it in your lifetime? I'm certain that you desire to. I'm sure you *hope* you will. But will you actually do it? What odds would you give yourself? One in five? One in a hundred? One in a million? How can you tell whether your chances are good or whether your dream will always remain exactly that—a dream? And are you willing to put it to the test?

Most people I know have a dream. In fact, I've asked hundreds, if not thousands, of people about their dream. Some willingly describe it with great detail and enthusiasm. Others are reluctant to talk about it. They seem embarrassed to say it out loud. These people have never tested their dream. They don't know if others will laugh at them. They're not sure if they're aiming too high or too low. They don't know if their dream is something they can really achieve or if they're destined to fail.

They have no idea how to achieve their dreams. What they possess is a vague notion that there is something they would like to do someday or someone they would like to become. But they don't know how to get from here to there. If that describes you, then you'll be glad to know that there really is hope. And I believe this book can help you.

KNOW THE ANSWERS BEFORE YOU TAKE THE TEST

When you were a kid in school, do you remember a teacher doing a review before a test and saying something like, "Pay attention now, because this is going to be on the test"? I do. The encouraging teachers who wanted to see their students succeed said things like that all the time. They wanted us to be prepared so that we could do well. They put us to the test, but they set us up for success.

My desire is to be like one of those encouraging teachers to you. I want to prepare you to put your dream to the test so that you can actually achieve it. How? I believe that if you know the right questions to ask yourself, and if you can answer these questions in an affirmative way, you will have an excellent chance of being able to achieve your dreams. The more questions you can answer positively, the greater the likelihood of success! That's the reason I wrote this book.

THE RIGHT AND WRONG PICTURE OF A DREAM

I've studied successful people for almost forty years. I've known hundreds of high-profile people who achieved big dreams. And I've achieved a few dreams of my own. What I've discovered is that a lot of people have misconceptions about dreams. Take a look at many of the things that people pursue and call dreams in their lives:

- **Daydreams**—Distractions from Current Work
- **Pie-in-the-Sky Dreams**—Wild Ideas with No Strategy or Basis in Reality
- **Bad Dreams**—Worries that Breed Fear and Paralysis

- **Idealistic Dreams**—The Way the World Would Be If You Were in Charge
- **Vicarious Dreams**—Dreams Lived Through Others
- **Romantic Dreams**—Belief that Some Person Will Make You Happy
- **Career Dreams**—Belief that Career Success Will Make You Happy
- **Destination Dreams**—Belief that a Position, Title, or Award Will Make You Happy
- **Material Dreams**—Belief that Wealth or Possessions Will Make You Happy

If these aren't good dreams—valid ones worthy of a person's life—then what are? Here is my definition of a dream that can be put to the test and pass: *a dream is an inspiring picture of the future that energizes your mind, will, and emotions, empowering you to do everything you can to achieve it.* A dream worth pursuing is a picture and blueprint of a person's purpose and potential. Or as my friend Sharon Hull says, "A dream is the seed of possibility planted in the soul of a human being, which calls him to pursue a unique path to the realization of his purpose."

WHAT DO YOU HAVE IN MIND?

Dreams are valuable commodities. They propel us forward. They give us energy. They make us enthusiastic. Everyone ought to have a dream. But what if you're not sure whether you have a dream you want to pursue? Let's face it. Many people were not encouraged to dream. Others have dreams but lose hope and set them aside.

I want you to know that there's good news. You can find or recapture your dreams. And they can be big dreams, not that all dreams have to be huge to be worth pursuing. They just need to be bigger than you are. As actress Josie Bisset remarked, "Dreams come a size too big so that we can grow into them."

> *"Dreams come a size too big so that we can grow into them."*
> —JOSIE BISSET

If you've given up hope, lost sight of your dream, or never connected with something that you think is worth dreaming and working toward, perhaps it would help you to learn about the five most common reasons that people have trouble identifying their dream:

1. SOME PEOPLE HAVE BEEN DISCOURAGED FROM DREAMING BY OTHERS

Many people have had their dreams knocked right out of them! The world is filled with dream crushers and idea killers. Some people who aren't pursuing any dreams of their own don't like to see others pursuing theirs. Other people's success makes them feel inadequate or insecure.

Business professors Gary Hamel and C. K. Prahalad wrote about an experiment conducted with a group of monkeys. Four monkeys were placed in a room that had a tall pole in the center. Suspended from the top of that pole was a bunch of bananas. One of the hungry monkeys started climbing the pole to get something to eat, but just as he reached out to grab a banana, he was doused with a torrent of cold water. Squealing, he scampered down the pole and abandoned his attempt to feed himself. Each monkey made a similar attempt, and each one was drenched with cold water. After making several attempts, they finally gave up.

Then researchers removed one of the monkeys from the room and replaced him with a new monkey. As the newcomer began to climb the pole, the other three grabbed him and pulled him down to the ground. After trying to climb the pole several times and being dragged down by the others, he finally gave up and never attempted to climb the pole again.

The researchers replaced the original monkeys, one by one, with new ones, and each time a new monkey was brought in, he would be dragged down by the others before he could reach the bananas. In time, only monkeys who had never received a cold shower were in the room, but none of them would climb the pole. They prevented one another from climbing, but none of them knew why.[1]

Perhaps others have dragged you down in life. They've discouraged you from dreaming. Maybe they resented the fact that you wanted to move up or to do something significant with your life. Or maybe they were trying to protect you from pain or disappointment. Either way, if you've been discouraged from dreaming, take heart. It's never too late to start dreaming and pursuing your dreams.

2. Some People Are Hindered by Past Disappointments and Hurts

Disappointment is the gap that exists between expectation and reality. All of us have encountered that gap. We've had unexpectedly bad experiences. We've had to live with our unfulfilled desires and we've had our hopes dashed. Disappointments can be highly damaging to us. Novelist Mark Twain observed, "We should be careful to get out of an experience only the wisdom that is in it—and stop there; lest we be like the cat that sits down on a hot stove-lid. She will never sit down on a hot stove-lid again—and that is well; but also she will never sit down on a cold one anymore."[2]

> *Disappointment is the gap that exists*
> *between expectation and reality.*

Haven't you found that to be true? When something goes wrong, we say, "I'll never do that again!" What a mistake, especially when it comes to our dreams! Failure is the price we must pay to achieve success. Some people must face failure repeatedly before they move forward in the pursuit of their dreams. Margaret Thatcher, former British Prime Minister asserted, "You may have to fight a battle more than once to win it." We need to remember that and make sure we don't give up the fight too soon.

3. Some People Get in the Habit of Settling for Average

Columnist Maureen Dowd says, "The minute you settle for less than you deserve, you get even less than you settled for." Dreams require a person to stretch, to go beyond average. You can't reach for a dream and remain safely mediocre at the same time. The two are incompatible.

When we are too uninspired to dream, when we settle for average, we may be tempted to blame it on others, on our circumstances, on the system. But the truth is that mediocrity is always a personal choice. D. Bruce Lockerbie, chairman and CEO of PAIDEIA, Inc., and former Thomas F. Staley Foundation scholar-in-residence at the Stony Brook School in New York, writes:

> Mediocrity isn't at root a national problem nor a corporate or institutional problem; nor a departmental problem; mediocrity is a personal problem. American education isn't a monolith, American education is made of millions of students being taught by millions of teachers, assisted by millions of supporting staff, equipped by millions of manufacturers and editors and suppliers—all paid for by billions of dollars! Each of these facets of American education is peopled by individuals. Therefore, *American education* isn't mediocre; but those of us who make decisions and appropriate funding for education may have been slipshod in our commitment to our work. *Schools* aren't mediocre; but some of us who are administrators or teachers, and our students, have been half-hearted about our management, our teaching, their learning. You see, *mediocrity* is first, a personal trait, a personal concession to less than our best, an individual lethargic resignation that says, "I guess good enough is good enough." Soon mediocrity metastasizes throughout the body politic, causing the nation to be at risk; but always remember, mediocrity begins with *me!*[3]

People who don't possess compelling dreams are in danger of having their lives merely slip away. Their days can become mundane, and then they become like their days. Author Kenneth Hildebrand expresses the negative effect of such an existence. He explains:

> The poorest of all men is not the one without a nickel to his name. He is the fellow without a dream.... [He is like] a great ship made for the mighty ocean but trying to navigate in a millpond. He has no far port to reach, no lifting horizon, no precious cargo to carry. His hours are absorbed in routine and petty tyrannies. Small wonder if he gets dissatisfied, quarrelsome and "fed up." One of life's greatest tragedies is a person with a 10-by-12 capacity and a two-by-four soul.[4]

If you feel that your life is closer to average than you desire, you need to do more dreaming. Nothing helps to break someone out of a rut like a worthwhile dream.

4. SOME PEOPLE LACK THE CONFIDENCE NEEDED TO PURSUE THEIR DREAMS

It takes confidence to talk about a dream and even more to pursue it. And sometimes confidence separates the people who dream and pursue those dreams from those who don't. In her research at the University of Wisconsin, Karen Greno-Malsch discovered that self-confidence is vital to success. In a study of children, she found that lower self-worth translated into 37 percent less willingness to negotiate and the use of 11 percent fewer negotiation strategies with others. She also discovered that the greater a child's self-worth, the greater the willingness to incur the risks of prolonged negotiation and the greater the adaptability. In other words, the more confidence you have in yourself, the less likely you are to give up trying to get what you want.[5]

Dreams are fragile. And they are at greatest risk when they are new to you, when people you love and respect don't approve of them, and when you have no past record of success to give you confidence. But confidence based on reality is necessary to strive for your dream. How do you gain such confidence? Through self-knowledge. Management consultant Judith Bardwick affirms that "real confidence comes from knowing and accepting yourself—your strengths and your limitations—in contrast to depending on the affirmation of others, from the outside." That's why I believe *Put Your Dream to the Test* can help you. Answering the questions positively will give you more confidence to pursue your dreams.

5. SOME PEOPLE LACK THE IMAGINATION TO DREAM

How do people discover their dreams? By dreaming! That may sound overly simplistic, but that's where it starts. Imagination is the soil that brings a dream to life. Nobel Prize–winning physicist Albert Einstein, a dreamer and thinker, understood the value of the imagination. He said, "When I examine myself and my methods of thought, I come to the conclusion that the gift of fantasy has meant more to me than my talent for absorbing positive knowledge." Einstein called his imagination a "holy curiosity."

> *Imagination is the soil that brings a dream to life.*

If you come from a discouraging background, or you don't think of yourself as an especially imaginative person, don't lose hope. You can still discover and develop a dream. God has put that ability in every one of us. If you know and watch children, then you know that's true. Every child dreams. Every child possesses imagination. My wife, Margaret, and I have five grandchildren, and whenever we are with them, we see their vivid imaginations at work, whisking them away from this world to ones of their own creation.

You have it in you to dream. Author and friend Max Lucado is clear about your possibilities: "You aren't an accident. You weren't mass produced. You aren't an assembly-line product. You were deliberately planned, specifically gifted, and lovingly positioned on the Earth by the Master Craftsman."[6] Beyond that, some people would even argue that the more drab your beginnings, the greater your potential for dreaming. Businessman Howard Schultz, who came from a very humble background, used the fertile soil of his imagination to help him cultivate the idea of Starbucks, the company he founded. Schultz says:

> One thing I've noticed about romantics: They try to create a new and better world from the drabness of everyday life. That is Starbuck's aim, too. We try to create, in our stores, an oasis, a little neighborhood spot where you can take a break, listen to some jazz, or ponder universal or personal or even whimsical questions over a cup of coffee.
>
> Who dreams up such a place?
>
> From my personal experience, I'd say that the more uninspiring your origins, the more likely you are to use your imagination and invent worlds where everything seems possible.
>
> That's certainly true of me.[7]

I believe God wants us to dream, and to dream big, because He's a big God who wants to do big things and He wants to do them through us. My friend Dale Turner asserts, "Dreams are renewable. No matter what our age or condition, there are still untapped possibilities within us and new beauty waiting to be born." It's never too late to dream.

ARE YOU READY TO PUT YOUR DREAM TO THE TEST?

Okay, you may be saying to yourself, *I've got a dream. I think it's worth pursuing. Now what? How can I know that my odds are good for achieving it?* That brings us to the questions, which comprise the ten chapters of this book. Here they are:

1. The Ownership Question: Is my dream really my dream?
2. The Clarity Question: Do I clearly see my dream?
3. The Reality Question: Am I depending on factors within my control to achieve my dream?
4. The Passion Question: Does my dream compel me to follow it?
5. The Pathway Question: Do I have a strategy to reach my dream?
6. The People Question: Have I included the people I need to realize my dream?
7. The Cost Question: Am I willing to pay the price for my dream?
8. The Tenacity Question: Am I moving closer to my dream?
9. The Fulfillment Question: Does working toward my dream bring satisfaction?
10. The Significance Question: Does my dream benefit others?

I believe that if you really explore each question, examine your-self honestly, and answer yes to all of them, the odds of your achieving your dream are very good. The more yeses you can answer, the more on target you are to fulfill your dreaming. I truly believe that everyone has the potential to imagine a worthwhile dream, and most have the ability to achieve it. And it doesn't matter how big or how seemingly outrageous your dream appears to others if your answers are yes to the Dream Test questions.

> *"Always remember there are only two kinds of people in this world—the realists and the dreamers. The realists know where they're going. The dreamers have already been there."*
> —ROBERT ORBEN

Speechwriter and comedy author Robert Orben asserted, "Always remember there are only two kinds of people in this world—the realists and the dreamers. The realists know where they're going. The dreamers have already been there." If you're a dreamer who has already been there in your mind, then the next step is to put your dream to the test. On the next several pages, you will find a Dream Test. It is designed to help you measure how prepared you currently are to reach your dream. I strongly recommend that you take the test before reading the rest of the book. The more work you can do to test your dream and to prepare before actually launching out to accomplish it, the greater the chance you will actually see your dream come true.

THE DREAM TEST

To assist you in putting your dream to the test, I've developed this Dream Test. Respond to each of the three statements under the dream questions by answering true or false. Once you've completed the test, enlist three people who know you well to help you evaluate yourself. If you have not already told them your dream, do so now. Then ask them to answer each of the questions as it applies to you. In addition, ask them to give you an overall score from 1 (not a chance) to 10 (absolute certainty) for how likely you are to achieve your dream.

1. The Ownership Question: Is my dream really my dream?

A. I would be the person in the world most pleased if I accomplished my dream.

B. I have publicly shared my dream with other people, including those I love.

C. My dream has been challenged by others, and I still embrace it.

2. The Clarity Question: Do I clearly see my dream?

A. I can explain the main gist of my dream in a single sentence.

B. I could answer nearly any question about the *what* (if not the *how*) of my dream.

C. I have written a clear description of my dream that includes its main features or objectives.

3. The Reality Question: Am I depending on factors within my control to achieve my dream?

A. I know what my greatest talents are, and my dream relies heavily on them.

B. My current habits and daily practices strongly contribute to the potential success of my dream.

C. My dream is likely to come true even if I am unlucky, if important people ignore or oppose me, or if I encounter serious obstacles.

4. The Passion Question: Does my dream compel me to follow it?

A. I can think of nothing I would rather do more than see my dream fulfilled.

B. I think about my dream every day and often wake up or fall asleep thinking about it.

C. This dream has been consistently important to me for at least a year.

5. The Pathway Question: Do I have a strategy to reach my dream?

A. I have a written plan for how I intend to accomplish my dream.

B. I have shared my plan with three people I respect to get their feedback.

C. I have made significant changes to my priorities and work habits to put my plan into action.

6. The People Question: Have I included the people I need to realize my dream?

A. I have surrounded myself with people who inspire me and who are honest with me about my strengths and weaknesses.

B. I have recruited people with complementary skills to help me accomplish my dream.

C. I have transferred the vision for my dream to others, and they share ownership for it.

7. The Cost Question: Am I willing to pay the price for my dream?

A. I can recount specific costs I have already paid toward achieving my dream.

B. I have already considered what I am willing to trade to achieve my dream.

C. I will not be compromising my values, ruining my health, or damaging my family to pursue my dream.

8. The Tenacity Question: Am I moving closer to my dream?

A. I can identify obstacles I have already overcome in the pursuit of my dream.

B. I do something every day—even if it's very small—to move closer to my dream.

C. I am willing to do extraordinarily difficult things to grow and change so that I can accomplish my dream.

9. The Fulfillment Question: Does working toward my dream bring satisfaction?

A. I am willing to give up my idealism in order to make my dream become reality.

B. I am willing to work for years or even decades to achieve my dream because it is that important to me.

C. I enjoy the pursuit of my dream so much that even if I fail, I will consider my life to have been well spent.

10. The Significance Question: Does my dream benefit others?

A. I can name specific people other than myself who will benefit if my dream is realized.

B. I am working to build a team of like-minded people to accomplish my dream.

C. What I'm doing to achieve my dream will matter in five, twenty, or one hundred years.

If you are able to mark every statement as true, then the odds are very good that you will see your dream come to fruition. If you marked as false one or more of the statements under a question, then you need to examine whether you are being honest with yourself about where you stand related to that question. Spend time in reflection, and do the exercises at the end of that question's chapter.

You should also talk to the three people who evaluated these questions related to you. Did their answers match yours? If not, ask for their observations. Also take a look at their overall score for you. If they gave you less than a ten, ask, "What would it take for me to make it a ten?" Listen, take notes, ask clarifying questions, but do not defend yourself. As you receive their answers, look for patterns, and remember what management consultant Jack Rosenblum says: "If one person tells you you're a horse, they're crazy. If three people tell you you're a horse, there is a conspiracy afoot. If ten people tell you you're a horse, it's time to buy a saddle."

CHAPTER 1

The Ownership Question
Is My Dream Really My Dream?

Whatever you think, be sure it is what you think;
whatever you want, be sure that it is what you want;
whatever you feel, be sure that it is what you feel.

–T. S. Eliot

His father wanted him to become a policeman. After all, his father was the chief of police in the small town where he grew up. His mother had other ideas. She believed he should become a carpenter. She saw that he didn't have much interest or aptitude for academic subjects in school, and she wanted him to learn a practical trade. At her request, Arnold dutifully enrolled in a carpentry apprenticeship program while in high school, but his heart was never really in it.

WHOSE DREAM IS IT?

Many young people find themselves in this kind of situation when they are growing up. They don't know what they're good at. They don't know what they want to do. So they listen to their parents or friends and start in a direction for their lives that reflects someone else's desires and dreams, not their own. And that shouldn't be a surprise. Children first see themselves through the eyes of their parents and other role models. They have no other point of reference. Counseling expert Cecil G. Osborne, in *The Art of Understanding Yourself*, observes, "The young child has no clear picture of himself. He sees himself only in the mirror of his parents' evaluation of himself. . . . A child who is told repeatedly that he is a bad boy, or is lazy, or no good, or stupid, or shy, or clumsy, will tend to act out this picture which the parent or some other authority figure has given him."[1] Many young people lose touch with their emerging identity—who they are and what they would really like to do—and they adopt the dreams and desires of someone else's heart because they wish to gain approval or because they don't know what else to do.

Anytime you see people pursuing a midlife career change, you can almost be certain they had been living someone else's dream and lost their way.

How many people attend law school because that is what their parents want? How many get married to please their mother? How many get a "real job" instead of pursuing a career in movies or the theater? Anytime you see people pursuing a midlife career change, you can almost be certain they had been living someone else's dream and lost their way. As disruptive as such a transition can be, they are more fortunate than the people who never discover and pursue their own dreams.

Even encouraging, positive, well-meaning parents can steer their children in a wrong direction. I know because I experienced it in a small way when I was seven years old. My parents were convinced that I possessed musical talent. They bought a piano and signed me up for lessons. For a couple of years, I enjoyed learning and practicing. I didn't have a passion for it, but I kept playing because it brought joy to my mom and dad.

My parents decided to broaden my musical horizons when I reached the fifth grade, and they bought me a trumpet. My teacher informed them that my mouth was not shaped correctly for that instrument, so they switched me to the clarinet. A famous clarinet player named Ted Lewis had come from my hometown, Circleville, Ohio, so friends started saying, "Maybe you can become the next Ted Lewis!"

Not likely. I didn't even have enough talent to make first chair in my elementary school band. I was the *last* clarinet!

At that age I really wanted to play basketball. I can still remember the pressure and heaviness of heart I felt when I finally sat down with my parents to tell them that I wanted to give up music to play sports. I can also remember the exhilaration I felt as they let go of their dream for me to become a great musician. It was with great joy that I packed away my clarinet for good and picked up a basketball.

ARNOLD'S DREAM

Arnold wasn't sure of what he wanted to do, but he knew it wasn't law enforcement or carpentry. It wasn't for lack of trying to find his dream. He had ambition. In fact, one thing he did know was that he wanted to be the best in the world at whatever he chose. He loved athletics, but in his midteens, he still hadn't found the right sport. He had tried many: ice curling, boxing, running, and field events such as javelin and shot put. For five years, he played soccer but had no strong passion for it. Then one day his soccer coach asked members of the team to start lifting weights once a week to improve their conditioning. It was then that his dream began to take shape.

"I still remember that first visit to the bodybuilding gym," he recalls. "I had never seen anyone lifting weights before. Those guys were . . . powerful looking, Herculean. And there it was before me—my life, the answer I'd been seeking. It clicked. It was something I suddenly just seemed to reach out and find, as if I'd been crossing a suspended bridge and finally stepped off onto solid ground."[2]

At age fourteen, Arnold Schwarzenegger had found his passion in a gymnasium. His dream came just a few months later when he spotted a magazine in a store window. On its cover was the image of a bodybuilder playing the role of Hercules in a movie. Arnold remembers what happened next:

> I scraped up the *pfennigs* [Austrian pennies] that I had left and bought that magazine. It turned out that Hercules was an English guy [named Reg Park] who'd won the Mr. Universe title in bodybuilding and parlayed that into a movie career—then took the money and built a gym empire. Bingo! I had my role model! If he could do it, I could do it! I'd win Mr. Universe. I'd become a movie star. I'd get rich. One, two, three—bing, bang, boom! I found my passion. I got my goal.[3]

Not everyone understood Arnold's dream—certainly not his parents or the friends he grew up with. His father hoped it would be a passing phase.

"Well, Arnold, what do you want to do?" he would ask.

"Dad, I'm going to be a professional bodybuilder. I'm going to make it my life," Arnold would explain.

"I can see you're serious, but how do you plan to apply it?"[4]

No one understood Arnold's choice, his dedication, and his vision.

"I could not have chosen a less popular sport," Arnold explains. "My school friends thought I was crazy. But I didn't care. . . . I had found the thing to which I wanted to devote my total energies and there was no stopping me. My drive was unusual; I talked differently than my friends; I was hungrier for success than anyone I knew."[5] That's the power of a compelling dream. A dream is an inspiring picture of the future that energizes your mind, will, and emotions, empowering you to do everything you can to achieve it.

Once Arnold had found a dream of his own, he was relentless in its pursuit. He began working out for hours at a time, six days a week. His dream was to become the best built man in the world. At age eighteen while he served his mandatory year in the Austrian army, he won the Junior Mr. Europe, his first major competition. The next year he won Mr. Europe. He moved to Munich and kept working. He obtained part ownership in a gym there. And in 1967, he won the Mr. Universe amateur contest in London. He was only twenty years old, and his victory astounded everyone. When he called his parents to tell them about his success, they were less than excited.

"If it had been through the local Graz paper saying I had just completed my college degree, it would have meant more to them," remarks Arnold. "In a way I cared that they didn't understand it. I felt they ought to have at least realized what it meant to me. They knew how hard I had worked for it. . . . I think you're always doing things for the approval of your parents."[6]

Despite the lack of support for his career choice, Arnold went on to win every major bodybuilding competition in the world, including the prestigious Mr. Olympia contest an incredible seven times, the last in 1980. But becoming the world's greatest bodybuilder—an amazing accomplishment in itself—was not Arnold's only dream. Many people were shocked when he was able to turn his bodybuilding prowess into a successful movie career. Years later, they were flabbergasted when he ran for governor of California—and won. What most people didn't know was that Arnold had dreamed of such things since his early days in Austria. At age twenty, he told a friend, "I want to win the Mr. Universe many times like Reg [Park, his idol]. I want to go into films like Reg. I want to be a billionaire. And I want to go into politics."[7]

Arnold has lived his dream. He became Mr. Universe and Mr. Olympia many times. He's made many movies, with his films earning more than $1.6 billion![8] He's been a highly successful businessperson. Since the early days in the United States, he's been a disciplined saver and wise investor in real estate, stocks, and businesses. (He's not quite a billionaire yet; it's estimated that his net worth is *only* $800 million.)[9] He is a political leader. Arnold Schwarzenegger has owned his dream, and as a result, he has been highly successful.

"From the very beginning I knew bodybuilding was the perfect choice for my career," says Arnold. "No one else seemed to agree—at least not my family or teachers. To them the only acceptable way of life was being a banker, secretary, doctor, or salesman—being established in the ordinary way, taking the regular kind of job offered through an employment agency—something legitimate. My desire to build my body and be Mr. Universe was totally beyond their comprehension."[10] But it wasn't beyond Arnold's comprehension—or his ability to achieve it because he was able to answer the Ownership Question affirmatively.

A DREAM IS POSSIBLE ONLY IF YOU OWN IT

How do you answer the Ownership Question? Is your dream really *your* dream? Are you willing to put it to the test? In the name of being sensible, many people ignore their desires. They undertake a career to please their parents, their spouses, or others. That may make them dutiful, but it will not make them successful. You cannot achieve a dream that you do not own.

> *You cannot achieve a dream that you do not own.*

Think about your personal history. How have your plans, goals, and desires been influenced by others? Are you aware of how your vision for yourself has been impacted? Is it possible that your dreams are the result of . . .

> Who your parents think you are?
> Who others think you are?
> Who you wish you were?
>
> Or are they the result of . . .
> Who you really are and are meant to be?

It is the responsibility of every individual to sort that out for himself or herself. In fact, you will fulfill your dream and live the life for which God created you *only* after you figure it out. As Nobel Prize winner for literature Joseph Brodsky observed, "One's task consists first of all in mastering a life that is one's own, not imposed or prescribed from without, no matter how noble its appearance may be. For each of us is issued but one life, and we know full well how it all ends. It would be regrettable to squander this one chance on someone else's appearance, someone else's experience."[11]

How do you know whether you're pursuing a dream that's not really *your* dream? Here are some clues to help you figure it out:

WHEN SOMEONE ELSE OWNS YOUR DREAM	WHEN YOU OWN YOUR DREAM
It will not have the right fit.	It will feel right on you.
It will be a weight on your shoulders.	It will provide wings to your spirit.
It will drain your energy.	It will fire you up.
It will put you to sleep.	It will keep you up at night.
It will take you out of your strength zone.	It will take you out of your comfort zone.
It will be fulfilling to others.	It will be fulfilling to you.
It will require others to make you do it.	You will feel you were made to do it.

> *When the dream is right for the person and the person is right for the dream, the two cannot be separated from each other.*

When the dream is right for the person and the person is right for the dream, the two cannot be separated from each other. For something to truly be your dream, you need to see the possibility it

You must take responsibility for your dream

represents—and you need to own it! Philosopher Søren Kierkegaard asserted, "A possibility is a hint from God. One must follow it."

Ownership is the first vital step to fulfilling a dream. It is like the key that opens a dream to everything else. When you own your dream, don't you see it more clearly? When you own it, don't you rely on things you can control to achieve it? Doesn't your passion increase, and aren't you more likely to develop a strategy to achieve it? Don't you include other people in it and pay the price to achieve it? When you own your dream, don't you become more tenacious and fulfilled while pursuing it? Doesn't its significance increase? All the other questions about your dream are more easily answered in the affirmative once you take ownership for it.

I HAVE A DREAM, BUT . . .

Most people don't live out their dreams. They wish and wait. They make excuses. They hope for the best. As time goes by and their dreams are unfulfilled, some become frustrated and bitter. Others give up. Author and thinker Henry David Thoreau stated, "The mass of men lead lives of quiet desperation." I believe one of the reasons so few people realize their dreams is that they don't take responsibility for them.

My brother, Larry, has often reminded me of the importance of putting a stake in the game for any endeavor. By a *stake in the game*, he means investing something of value. Anytime that happens, a person's level of commitment goes way up. Why? Because if you own something, you must give it energy, money, time, and commitment. When you have a stake in the game, you no longer have an easy come, easy go attitude about it. You are invested in it. Whenever Larry goes

[handwritten note: Excuses people have for not following THEIR dreams]

into a business deal with someone, he is sure that both have a stake in the game, or he doesn't move forward.

You need to possess a similar attitude about your dream. You need to have a stable in it, to own it. When you do, you become empowered to rise above the excuses offered by people for not pursuing a dream, such as the following three I hear most often:

Excuse #1: Dreams Don't Come True for Ordinary People

Many people believe that dreams are only for special people, and everyone else has to settle for less. But I disagree with that mind-set. It is true that the people who shape history have dreams. The Wright brothers wanted to fly. Winston Churchill envisioned a free Europe. Martin Luther King, Jr. dreamed about racial equality. However, you don't have to be a world figure to have a dream. Everyone can have a dream and pursue it. In fact, the pursuit of a dream often makes the difference between ordinary and extraordinary people. Ordinary people can live extraordinary lives when they follow their dreams. Why do I say that? Because a dream becomes a catalyst to help people make important changes in their lives. You don't just change who you are in order to live out your dream. You pursue your dream, and the process changes who you are and what you can accomplish. A dream is both a target and a catalyst.

Excuse #2: If the Dream Isn't Big, It's Not Worth Pursuing

A dream should never be evaluated according to its size. That's not what determines its worth. A dream doesn't have to be big. It just has to be bigger than you are.

My friend Dan Reiland told me about a member of his staff who told his colleagues, "All I ever wanted to be was a great dad." They didn't criticize him because he wasn't shooting for the moon. And as he talked to them about his heartfelt desire, he had everyone in tears. It wasn't a big dream, but it was a powerful one. Bigger is not always better, and size does not determine significance.

Excuse #3: Now Is Not the Right Time to Pursue My Dream

The most common excuse for not owning and pursuing a dream is timing. Some say it's too soon. They wait for permission to go after their dream—permission that can be given to them only by themselves. Meanwhile, the few, like Arnold Schwarzenegger, see their dream and go after it, affirming the words of author Pearl S. Buck: "The young do not know enough to be prudent, and therefore they attempt the impossible, and achieve it, generation after generation."

> *"The young do not know enough to be prudent, and therefore they attempt the impossible, and achieve it, generation after generation."*
> —Pearl S. Buck

Others fear that it's too late for them to pursue their dreams. As a result, they give up. But I believe that novelist George Eliot was right when she said, "It's never too late to be what you might have been."

Movie star Jim Carrey met challenges and discouragement early in his career as a stand-up comedian. He explains that when he felt like giving up on his dream to make it in the entertainment industry, he would think about Rodney Dangerfield, who struggled for decades before he reached the top of his profession. "I did stand-up in clubs for fifteen years," recalls Carrey, "and sometimes the only thing that kept me going was the thought that Rodney had dropped out of the business when he was thirty but had come back and made it big when he was in his forties. Made it big. In a business that almost always values youth over talent, he was . . . absolute proof that it's never too late to make your mark. You may have to quit for a while and sell some aluminum siding, but you don't have to give up your dreams."[12] The timing will never be perfect for you to pursue your dream, so you might as well start now. If you don't, then next year you'll be a year older and not a step closer to it.

HOW TO TAKE OWNERSHIP OF YOUR DREAM

If you're willing to take that step—to start owning your dream—then begin the process by doing the following:

1. BE WILLING TO BET ON YOURSELF

You may succeed if nobody else believes in you, but you will never succeed if you don't believe in yourself. In fact, if you can't believe in yourself, you will have a difficult time believing in much of anything else. You will be adrift in the world with nothing compelling you to move forward. However, people who take ownership of their dreams believe in themselves, and when they believe in themselves, they are willing to bet on themselves.

> *You may succeed if nobody else believes in you, but you will never succeed if you don't believe in yourself.*

Owning a dream means having your belief in yourself outweigh your fears. A scene in the movie *Akeelah and the Bee* illustrates the power of believing in yourself and what you are capable of doing. The story is about Akeelah, a girl from South Los Angeles who overcomes many obstacles to compete at the National Spelling Bee. When her spelling coach, Dr. Larabee (played by Laurence Fishburne), asks her, "Have you got any goals? What would you like to be when you grow up? A doctor, a lawyer, a stand-up comic?" she responds, "I don't know. The only thing I'm good at is spelling."

"Go over there," he says, motioning toward a plaque, "and read the quotation that's on the wall. Read it aloud please."

She reads, "Our deepest fear is not that we are inadequate. Our deepest fear is that we are powerful beyond measure. We ask ourselves, 'Who am I to be brilliant, gorgeous, talented, and fabulous?' Actually, who are you *not* to be? We were born to make manifest the glory of God that is within us. And as we let our own light shine, we unconsciously give other people permission to do the same."[13]

"Does that mean anything to you?" Larabee asks. "What does it mean?"

"That I'm not supposed to be afraid," she answers.

"Afraid of what?"

"Afraid of . . . me?"[14]

You will never believe in your dream unless you first believe in yourself. I can recall hearing this comment on the idea:

> I create big ideas because I believe I can, not because I am creative. At the top of the pyramid one has the power to create anything and create value for everything created. My climb began as a child, helped by my parents and teachers, and continued through the help of my mentors and my wife and children. All these people added to my psychological capital. The bottom line is this: A healthy self-worth creates a wealthy net worth.

If you want to succeed, you need to believe that you can. You must bet on yourself if you want to see your dreams come true.

2. Lead Your Life Instead of Just Accepting Your Life

The power of choice is the greatest power that a person possesses. Unfortunately, many people just accept their lives—they don't become leaders of themselves. As a result, they can't get out of their own way.

Choosing to lead your life and not just accepting it is critical to owning your dream. Holocaust survivor Elie Wiesel wrote in *Souls on Fire* that when you die and you go to meet your Maker, you're not going to be asked why you didn't become a messiah or find a cure for cancer. All you're going to be asked is, "Why didn't you become you? Why didn't you become all that you are?" Reaching your God-given potential requires taking responsibility for yourself and your life. It means taking an active leadership role with yourself.

How do you do that? By saying yes—to yourself, to hope, to your dream. Every time you say yes, you open yourself up to your potential and to greater possibilities. If you're used to saying no, you may find it difficult. If that is true in your case, then at least be willing to say maybe to yourself. Never forget that you are a miracle, that you are unique, possessing talents, experiences, and opportunities that no one else has ever had—or ever will have. It is your responsibility to become everything that you are, not only for your benefit but also for everyone else's.

3. LOVE WHAT YOU DO AND DO WHAT YOU LOVE

Irving Berlin was one of the most prolific and successful composers in American history. He wrote songs such as "God Bless America," "Easter Parade," and "I'm Dreaming of a White Christmas," which still ranks as the all-time best-selling musical score. In an interview reported in the *San Diego Union*, Don Freeman asked Berlin, "Is there any question you've never been asked that you would like someone to ask you?"

"Well, yes, there is one," Berlin replied. "'What do you think of the many songs you've written that didn't become hits?' My reply would be that I still think they are wonderful."[15]

Successful people—those who see and seize their dream—love what they do and do what they love. They allow their passion and talent to guide them. Why? Because talent, purpose, and potential always come hand in hand. I don't believe that God makes mistakes. He doesn't create people to be talented in one area but interested in an unrelated one. There is always a potential alignment of talent and passion if we have the courage to pursue our purpose and take risks.

Po Bronson, author of *What Should I Do with My Life?* writes:

> I'm convinced that business success in the future starts with the question, What should I do with my life? Yes, that's right. . . . People don't succeed by migrating to a "hot" industry (one word: dotcom) or by adopting a particular career-guiding mantra (remember "horizontal careers"?). They thrive focusing on the question of who they really are—and connecting that to work that they truly love (and, so doing, unleashing a productive and creative power that they never imagined).[16]

Many successful people echo Bronson's assertion. Carly Fiorina, former chairman and CEO of Hewlett-Packard, advises, "Love what you do, or don't do it. Don't make a choice of any kind, whether in career or in life, just because it pleases others or because it ranks high on someone else's scale of achievement. . . . Make the choice to do something because it engages your heart as well as your mind. Make the choice because it engages all of you."[17] Don't become a slave to someone else's dream. Why? Because once you own a dream, it will also own you. Being a slave to someone else's dream will become a nightmare.

4. Don't Compare Yourself (or Your Dream) to Others

Everyone I know wants to be successful, but nearly everybody defines *success* differently. How do you define it? Do you agree with *Webster's*, which offers as one of its definitions: "The gaining of wealth, fame, rank, etc."?[18] If you do, then how much wealth is enough to be successful? How much fame? Should you pick an arbitrary target? Should you compare yourself to others? And what if you have decided to devote yourself to raising children of character or serving your community? Does that mean you're less successful than others who have achieved high rank or monetary advantages? I don't think so.

Success is doing the best you can with what you have wherever you start in life. You should never let others set the standard for you, just as you should never try to live someone else's dream. Comparing ourselves to others doesn't benefit us, nor does it get us any closer to living our dream. When we play the comparison game, we're like the cows in the pasture that see a milk truck go by with a sign that says, "Pasteurized, homogenized, standardized, Vitamin A added." One cow says to the other, "Makes you feel sort of inadequate, doesn't it?"

> *Success is doing the best you can with what you have wherever you start in life.*

Author and friend Joyce Meyer wisely states, "God will help you be all you can be, but He will never help you be someone else." If you focus too much attention on who you *aren't* by comparing yourself to someone else, you lose sight of who you need to become. Now that I have passed sixty years of age, I can tell you with certainty that there is great wisdom in the 18/40/60 Rule. When you're 18, you worry about what everybody is thinking about you. When you're 40, you don't give a darn what anybody thinks of you. When you're 60, you realize that nobody has been thinking about you at all!

5. Believe in Your Vision for the Future Even When Others Don't Understand You

You are not an accident. You are here for a reason. Ralph Waldo Emerson asserted, "Self-trust is the first secret of success, the belief that if you are here the authorities of the universe put you here, and for cause, or with some task strictly appointed you in your constitution, and so long as you work at that you are well and successful."

Though you have great potential and the seed of purpose in you, others will not necessarily understand you. Like Arnold Schwarzenegger, you may see an image of what your future could be, yet others might see an arrogant or presumptive person. Don't let that dissuade you from taking ownership of your dream and moving forward.

Journalist Anna Quindlen, who won a Pulitzer Prize in 1992, had a dream in her heart and a vision for the future that took her down a road that others couldn't understand. In an address to the class of 2002 at Sarah Lawrence College, Quindlen explained, "When I quit the *New York Times* to be a full-time mother, the voices of the world said I was nuts. When I quit the paper again to be a novelist, they said I was nuts again. But if success is not on your own terms, if it looks good to the world but does not feel good in your soul, it is not success at all."[19]

If your dream is really your dream, then it will seem outrageous to more than a few people. Now I'm not saying your dream can ignore reality, which is something I address in the Reality Question (chapter 3). What I'm saying is that you will undoubtedly have to overcome some naysayers to achieve your dream. And if someone tries to silence your hopes or deny your progress to pursue your dream, maybe that person isn't your friend.

> *"If success is not on your own terms,*
> *if it looks good to the world but does not feel good*
> *in your soul, it is not success at all."*
> —ANNA QUINDLEN

Everyone has the potential to live way beyond average. As Robert Kriegel and Louis Patler write in *If It Ain't Broke . . . Break It!,* "We don't have a clue as to what people's limits are. All the tests, stopwatches, and finish lines in the world can't measure human potential. When someone is pursuing their dream, they'll go far beyond what seems to be their limitations. The potential that exists within us is limitless and largely untapped . . . when you think of limits, you create them."[20]

GRAB HOLD OF YOUR DREAM

Dreams have enormous power. Mary Shelley, author of *Frankenstein,* remarked, "My dreams were all my own. I accounted for them to nobody. They were my refuge when annoyed—my dearest pleasure when free." If you have a dream and are not trying to live it, then the first place you need to look to find out why is inside yourself. Either you are nurturing a dream that really isn't your own, or you are not taking ownership of the dream you have.

God has put a dream inside you. It's yours, and no one else's. It declares your uniqueness. It holds your potential. Only you can birth it. Only you can live it. Not to discover it, take responsibility for it, and act upon it is to negatively affect yourself as well as all those who would benefit from your dream.

Poet John Greenleaf Whittier wrote, "For all sad words of tongue and pen, the saddest are these, 'It might have been.'" When you are in your twilight years and you're looking back on your life, will you sense that you lived life to the fullest, striving to fulfill your purpose and realize your dream? Or will you feel that you lived merely to fulfill the expectations of your parents or spouse or friends? What will you have done with this gift of life? If you think that question will be important then, it should be important to you now. The first step in being able to answer it is to take ownership of your dream and prepare to start moving forward.

CAN YOU ANSWER YES TO
THE OWNERSHIP QUESTION:
IS MY DREAM REALLY MY DREAM?

If your answer to the Ownership Question isn't a resounding yes, then you need to do two things: (1) get better connected with yourself and your dreams, and (2) develop enough confidence to take ownership of it. To better understand yourself, answer the following questions:

1. What would I do if I had no limitations?
2. What would I do if I had only five years to live?
3. What would I do if I had unlimited resources?
4. What would I do if I knew I couldn't fail?

Once you have answered these questions thoughtfully and honestly, spend some time in quiet reflection to better understand your dream. When you believe you have discovered it, verify with people you trust that it is consistent with your talents, skills, and history. But beware! If you are surrounded by negative people who don't see your potential, they may not be adequate judges of your abilities.

If confidence is your problem, follow the advice of speaker and former Ohio state legislator Les Brown in his book *Live Your Dreams*. He suggests you ask yourself,

What are my gifts?
What are five things I like about myself?

What people make me feel special?

What moment of personal triumph do I remember?

He believes asking these questions will increase a person's self-approval. "Find out what it is you want and go after it as if your life depends on it," declares Brown. "Why? Because it does!"

CHAPTER 2

The Clarity Question
Do I Clearly See My Dream?

Give to us clear vision that we may
know where to stand and what to stand for.

—Peter Marshall

In the summer of 2007, Mike Hyatt and several other friends joined me in Ireland for a few days of golf. Mike has been in publishing since he was in college and has done just about everything in the industry at one time or another. He's been an author, an agent, a publisher, and even a publishing house founder. Mike is an exceptional leader. Today he serves as the president and CEO of Thomas Nelson, Inc.

I enjoy playing golf. Though I'm not much better than average as a golfer, I love being on beautiful courses, and I like the exercise. But I also believe that golf outings are great times to build relationships and to do some business. Early one morning in Ireland as I was talking to Mike, I showed him the working outline for *Put Your Dream to the Test*. After reading through it, he immediately said, "John, you have to include a chapter on the importance of a clear vision. If you don't have clarity, you don't have anything." And then he began telling me a story from his experience.

OPPORTUNITY OF A LIFETIME

In July 2000, Mike's boss at Thomas Nelson suddenly resigned. At that time, Mike was the associate publisher of Nelson Books, the trade book division of the company, and he was invited to take his former boss's job as publisher.

"I knew our division was in bad shape," Mike explains. "But I didn't know how bad things really were until I became the publisher. I took a deep breath and began to assess reality." Here's what Mike discovered:

- *His was the least profitable of fourteen divisions in the company.* In fact, his division had actually *lost* money the previous year. People in the other divisions were mumbling about how his division was negatively impacting the entire company.
- *Revenue growth for the division had been flat for three years.* In addition, they had just lost their single biggest author to a competing publishing company, making future revenue growth even less likely.
- *His division was the least efficient user of working capital at Thomas Nelson.* As a percentage of revenue, inventory and royalty advances were the highest in the company, but they provided virtually no return to shareholders.
- *Everyone in the division was exhausted.* The division was publishing 125 new titles a year with only ten employees. Everyone was overworked, and the quality of the work showed it.

Mike says, "Things could not have been worse. However, as the new divisional executive, I recognized that things could not have been better for me. It was a great career opportunity. If I turned the division around, I would be a hero. If I didn't, that would be okay too. After all, the division was a mess when I inherited it. I couldn't lose."

At that point, most executives would have launched into a major strategy session to dig the organization out of the hole it was in. Not Mike. Through the years, he had learned that when people think about the *how* too soon, they hurt their potential. It actually inhibits their dreaming and blocks them from thinking as big as they can. He knows that the accomplishment of a dream depends on the clarity of the vision.

"What you need is a vision that is so big that it is compelling," explains Mike, "not only to others, but to you. If it's not compelling, you won't have the motivation to stay the course, and you won't be able to recruit others to help you. Both vision and strategy are important, but there is a priority to them. Vision always comes first. Always. If you have a clear vision, you will eventually attract the right strategy. If you don't have a clear vision, no strategy will save you. I have seen this over and over again in my professional life and personal life."

> *"If you have a clear vision, you will eventually attract the right strategy. If you don't have a clear vision, no strategy will save you."*
> —MIKE HYATT

So what did Mike do to get a clear picture of what he wanted to accomplish?

"The first thing I did was to go on a private retreat," Mike says. "I had one objective in mind. I wanted to get crystal clear on my vision. What did I want to see happen? What would the division look like in three years? I didn't care about strategy; I was only concerned with vision. If I had been strategic before I was visionary, I might have said, 'Well, I don't see how we can accomplish much. The situation is so dire. We don't have many resources to work with. Let's just try to break even this next year. Maybe we can reduce our working capital some by selling off a little obsolete inventory. And maybe we can sign a few new authors and get a little revenue growth.'

"Do you think anyone would have gotten excited about this? Would this vision have attracted the right authors? Would it have retained the right employees? Would it have secured additional corporate resources? I don't think so. The problem is that people get stuck on the *how*. They don't see how they could accomplish more, so they throttle back their vision, convinced that they must be realistic. And what they expect becomes their new reality."

Mike was very wise. You have to identify the target before you try to hit it. You have to know what the landscape looks like before you can paint a picture of it to others. You have to see the dream with clarity before you can try to achieve it. If you don't clearly see your dream—or if you get bogged down in real or imaginary restrictions—you limit yourself. If you're going to dream, you might as well dream big. And that's what Mike did. During his retreat, he worked on a vision statement—something he would find compelling. After all, if he couldn't get excited about it, nobody else in his division would either. He gave himself permission to envision the perfect future. Then he wrote down a clear picture of his dream. This is what he wrote:

Vision Statement

Nelson Books is the world's largest,
most respected provider of inspirational books.

1. *We have ten franchise authors whose new books sell at least 100,000 copies in the first 12 months.*
2. *We have ten emerging authors whose new books sell at least 50,000 copies in the first 12 months.*
3. *We are publishing 60 new titles a year.*
4. *Authors are soliciting other authors on our behalf because they are so excited to be working with us.*
5. *The top agents routinely bring us their best authors and proposals because of our reputation for success.*
6. *We place at least four books a year on the* New York Times *bestsellers list.*
7. *We consistently have more books on the Christian bestsellers list than our competitors.*
8. *We consistently exceed our budget in revenue and margin contribution.*
9. *Our employees consistently max out their bonus plans.*
10. *We are the fastest-growing, most profitable division in our company.*

Mike's picture of the future was highly specific. That's the way to bring clarity to a dream!

When Mike returned to the office, he called a meeting with his entire staff. The first thing he did was to describe the current situation; he was brutally honest and didn't pull any punches. Then he shared his dream. And he described it in as much detail as he could.

Because his vision was clear, his people could see it. Because it was compelling, most of them found it compelling too. He could sense their excitement, and most people quickly got on board.

But simply casting vision for everyone else wasn't enough. Mike knew he needed to keep the vision clear in his mind continually, so he read his vision statement every day. He thought about it all the time. He prayed about it. And he dreamed about it.

People began asking him, "How in the world are you going to accomplish this?" At first, his answer was, "I'm not sure, but I am confident it is going to happen. Just watch." And as he kept himself focused on the vision, a strategy began to emerge. But still his main focus wasn't on the strategy. It was on the dream. Mike says, "I spent way more time—probably ten to one—focused on the *what* rather than the *how*."

Mike expected the transformation of the division to take at least three years. Amazingly, he and his team achieved an almost complete turnaround in a mere eighteen months. By then, they had exceeded almost every aspect of the vision.

"This didn't happen because we had a great business strategy," declares Mike. "It happened because we had a clear vision of what we wanted to achieve. That's where it started, and that's where you have to start if you want to experience a different reality than the one you have now. You have to get clear on what you want."

Since 2002, Nelson Books has consistently been the fastest growing, most profitable division at Thomas Nelson, Inc. It's been the home of most of the company's most successful authors, producing one bestseller after another. That was no accident. And it was no accident that Mike was promoted from head of that division to president and later CEO of the entire organization. Today Thomas

Nelson is the largest publisher of inspirational material in the world and the sixth largest publisher in the United States. And it continues to be highly successful, even as other companies in the industry face difficult times. Why? Because the dream that Mike and the rest of the people at Thomas Nelson have for the company is crystal clear!

IS YOUR DREAM IN FOCUS?

Do you clearly see your dream? A clear and compelling dream has rescued many a struggling organization. Dreams have given meaning and significance to the lives of many an individual. Everything Mike said about clear dreams resonated deeply with me. Every time in my life that I accomplished anything significant, the dream was very clear to me beforehand. I knew what I was striving for.

If you want to accomplish a dream, you will be able to do so only when you can see it clearly. You must define it before you can pursue it. Most people don't do that. Their dream remains a dream—something fuzzy and unspecific. As a result, they never achieve it.

Pursuing a dream that isn't clear would be like someone who loves cowboy movies launching out on a trip to the Western United States merely hoping to run into something interesting by driving in that direction. Instead, the person would need to turn that vague notion into specifics, saying something like, "I want to visit the National Cowboy and Western Heritage Museum in Oklahoma City, then travel to Arizona to see the O.K. Corral in Tombstone, visit Old Tucson to see where they filmed *Rio Bravo,* my favorite Western, and see beautiful Monument Valley, where movies such as *Stagecoach* and *Once upon a Time in the West* were filmed." Now that can be accomplished!

If you want to achieve your dream, you need to bring it into focus. As you work toward that, here are some things to keep in mind:

1. A Clear Dream Makes a General Idea Very Specific

When I ask people to describe their dream, many of them stammer and stumble, trying to put into words a vague notion they've nurtured but never defined. A dream that isn't clear won't help you get anywhere.

What do you want to accomplish? What do you want to experience? What do you want to contribute? Who do you want to become? In other words, what does success look like for *you*? If you don't define it, you won't be able to achieve it.

It sounds overly simple, but a primary reason that most people don't *get* what they want is that they don't *know* what they want. They haven't defined their dream in clear and compelling detail. As actor and author Ben Stein asserts, "The indispensable first step to getting the things you want out of life is this: decide what you want."

> *"The indispensable first step to getting the things you want out of life is this: decide what you want."*
> —Ben Stein

Deciding what you want requires you to be specific and make your goals measurable. For example, take a look at these vague notions put into more specific form:

GENERAL IDEA	SPECIFIC GOAL
I want to lose weight.	I will weigh 185 pounds by June 1.
I need to treat employees better.	I will honor someone at every Monday staff meeting.
I want to get out of debt.	I will pay off all credit card balances by December 31.
I'd like to learn a language.	I will study Chinese one hour a day this year.
I ought to get in shape.	I will swim for an hour every day.
I need to improve my leadership.	I will read one leadership book every month.

A dream doesn't have to be ephemeral. Even a really audacious one can be concrete. In the early 1960s, President John F. Kennedy made a big dream concrete when he said, "This nation should commit itself to achieving the goal, before this decade is out, of landing a man on the moon." Albert Siepert, former deputy director of launch operations at the Kennedy Space Center, stated, "The reason that NASA has succeeded is because NASA had a clear-cut goal, and expressed its goal." When you first begin to wonder about your potential and brainstorm your future, it's good to let yourself go and think big. But when it's time to start making your dream come true, you need to get specific.

Being specific doesn't necessarily mean having every little detail thought out before you move forward. That would be a mistake. The big idea needs to be clear. The rest unfolds as you move forward, and you make adjustments as you go. But you should try to be as specific as you can about the overarching dream.

For years I have encouraged leaders to add value to their

employees, build them up, and motivate them to help them succeed. Adding value to people is a natural gift for me. But it's not for many people, and I could see that some struggled with it. Because I longed to help others in this area, I realized I needed to be specific on the subject and write about it. The result was a book I wrote with Les Parrott titled *25 Ways to Win with People: How to Make Others Feel Like a Million Bucks.* It explains practices to help people add value to others. Now I'm not just encouraging people to add value; I'm helping them actually do it.

2. A CLEAR DREAM DOESN'T BECOME CLEAR WITHOUT EFFORT

It doesn't take much effort to let your mind drift and dream. However, it takes *great* effort to set your mind to the task of developing a clear and compelling dream. Mike Hyatt says that when he took his retreat to get a clear vision for his division, he went to a solitary place with just a pen and journal. He began the process by describing in writing the current reality he was facing. He was brutally honest, writing down everything he didn't like. Only then did he write out in detail what he wanted to see happen in the future—not just as a vague dream of success or improvement. He even wrote it in the present tense to make the dream more concrete and credible.

Take the effort to bring clarity to your dream using your own tools and method. If you're like Mike, you can go away to a cabin with nothing but pen and paper. I, on the other hand, need starters to get me thinking in the right direction. Maybe they can help you as well. Here are some essentials I bring to the task of clarifying my dream . . .

⊛ *Questions.* For me the whole process begins with questions I must ask myself. The dream is always rooted in the dreamer, in his or her experiences, circumstances, talents, and opportunities. I ask:

> What am I feeling?—What are my emotions telling me?
> What am I sensing?—What is my intuition telling me?
> What am I seeing?—What is happening around me?
> What am I hearing?—What are others saying?
> What am I thinking?—What do my intellect and
>   common sense say?

If I can get a good sense of where I am, what I know, and what I want, I'm on my way to clarifying my dream.

⊛ *Resources.* I rarely try to think, create, or dream in a vacuum. I'm a firm believer in tools that can help me. Sometimes that means reading a book, listening to a message on CD, watching a movie, or reading quotations. Other times it means having a photograph or an object in front of me to help me dream. More than once I've kept a photograph on the desk in my office for a year or longer to help me see a dream more clearly.

⊛ *Experiences.* Years ago when my dream was to build an influential church in America, I reinforced and clarified that vision by visiting congregations around the country that were already influential. I have also traveled to historic areas and visited the home of one of my heroes to inspire me. Such experiences help me dream bigger and with greater clarity.

⊛ *People.* When I dream, I think about people who have already been where I want to go. For three years I made appointments with leaders who were already doing what I dreamed of so that I could gain insight from them. Those interactions gave me confidence, inspired me to dream bigger, and sharpened the picture of my dream. Listening to people share the details of their journey can sometimes help you discover the details of yours.

If you have already discovered a process for bringing clarity to your dream, then use that. If you haven't, try mine. Or do as Mike Hyatt did. But however you approach the task, remember this: it's usually a process. A clear picture of a dream may come to you all at once, in lightning bolt fashion, but for most people it doesn't work that way. Most people need to keep working at it, clarifying it, redrawing it. If the process is difficult, that's no reason to give up. In fact, if it's too easy, maybe you're not dreaming big enough. Just keep working at it because a clear dream is worth fighting for.

3. A Clear Dream Affirms Your Purpose

If you've answered the Ownership Question to verify that your dream really is your dream, then working to clarify your dream should reinforce the work you've already done. Bringing your dream into focus should confirm the sense that you are going in the right direction, and it should strengthen your sense of purpose.

I've found this to be true in my life. In my effort to clarify my dream, I discovered that the more clearly I saw my dream, the more clearly I was able to see my purpose. That is true, I believe, because a person's dream and purpose are intertwined. God designs us to *want* to do what we are most capable of doing. Because of this, when I visited churches that were making an impact, something resonated within me. I felt that I belonged in such places. And when I interviewed the successful leaders in these churches, I sensed that I could become one too. In a way, it was an odd situation. I was fanning the flames of my imagination, making me dream even bigger, and at the same time it confirmed the reality that I was on the right track. I could see a picture of my dream, and I could see myself in the picture!

> *In my effort to clarify my dream, I discovered*
> *that the more clearly I saw my dream,*
> *the more clearly I was able to see my purpose.*

When your dream and your purpose are aligned, you know it. That was true for filmmaker Steven Spielberg. When he was in high school, he dreamed of directing movies. "I want to be a director," he told his father, Arnold.

"Well," his father told him, "if you want to be a director, you've got to start at the bottom; you've got to be a gofer and work your way up."

"No, Dad," the younger Spielberg replied. "The first picture I do, I'm going to be a director." And he was.

"That blew my mind," his father says. "That takes guts." Arnold Spielberg was so impressed with his son's ambition and confidence, he bankrolled Steven's first feature film, *Firelight*, a science fiction thriller that premiered at a little movie house in Phoenix, Arizona. During the making of the film, the young Spielberg told his collaborators, "I want to be the Cecil B. DeMille of science fiction."[1] That's not a bad description of what he has become, having produced or directed *Jurassic Park, Men in Black, Transformers, ET, Minority Report, Back to the Future, Gremlins, Close Encounters of the Third Kind,* and other science fiction films. Spielberg's dream was clear, and the power of that clarity helped him achieve it.

As you put your dream to the test and seek to bring clarity to it, having your dream and purpose aligned will change your life. Why? Because it will make clear why you're here on this earth. If you don't sense that alignment and strengthening of purpose, you might need to return to the Ownership Question and make sure your dream is really your dream.

4. A Clear Dream Determines Your Priorities

The Bridge on the River Kwai, which won the Academy Award for best picture in 1957, is considered by many to be one of the finest films ever made. The lead character, Colonel Nicholson, portrayed by Alec Guinness (who won the Academy Award as best actor that year) is a study in misplaced priorities. Nicholson is an admirable man and tough leader who is taken prisoner by the Japanese during World War II and finds himself the highest ranking officer in a Burmese prison camp. His Japanese captors try to coerce him into leading his fellow prisoners in the building of a railway bridge. In the beginning, Nicholson resists heroically, but in time he relents and begins the building project. Eventually he takes so much pride in the work his men are doing in the construction of the bridge that he loses sight of his real goal—defeating the Japanese and winning the war.

At the end of the movie, there is a moment when Nicholson actually starts to guard the bridge from attack by an Allied officer who has set charges to blow it up. But in a flash of insight during his dying breath, he says, "What have I done?" His last act is to detonate the explosives and blow up the bridge.

It's easy to get so caught up in the day-to-day process of life that you lose sight of the big picture. However, when your dream is clearly in sight, it helps you get your priorities straight.

Even though I've taught this truth for years, there are times when I need to be reminded of it. That was the case in December 2007 when I went to the hospital because I was experiencing some dizziness. After two days of tests, I learned that I had an irregular heartbeat.

Dr. Crandall, my new cardiologist, visited me in my hospital room to talk to me about my health. I knew what he was going to say. I hadn't been watching my diet for quite some time. So in an effort to show him that I knew what was coming, I said, "Dr. Crandall, I know I need to do some weight management."

"No, you don't need to do weight management," he replied, much to my surprise. For a moment I had hope. "You need to do weight *loss*. John, you're fat! After you lose a bunch of weight, *then* you can manage it!" During our fifteen-minute conversation, if he told me once, he told me a dozen times that I was fat. He was making sure he brought great *clarity* to the picture for me.

With my problem in focus and the dream of wanting to remain healthy so that I can continue to spend time with family, my priorities became clear. I would do what it took to reach a healthy weight. That meant changing my priorities and developing a new pattern for living, which would dictate what I did in the future. Until further notice, I would consume no more than sixteen hundred calories a day. And I would exercise for no less than one hour every day. If I wanted to achieve my dream of a long and healthy life, I would have to realign my living according to these priorities.

Nobody can have it all. We like to think we can, but we can't. If you see your dream clearly—and keep it in front of you continually —it will help you to understand what you must sacrifice and what you must dedicate yourself to in order to keep moving forward.

Only a clear picture of who you are and where you want to go can help you prioritize what you need to do. We all make choices. The question is, Are you going to make choices that bring you closer to your dream or take you farther away from it? If you don't know exactly what your dream is, then you won't be capable of making the right choices. Clarity of vision creates clarity of priorities.

Clarity of vision creates clarity of priorities.

5. A Clear Dream Gives Direction and Motivation to the Team

Your big dream will undoubtedly require the participation of other people. If you are part of an organization that has goals or vision, then you must work with other people in order to accomplish them. No matter what, you must be capable of working with a team. That can be done effectively only when you possess a clear picture of what you want to achieve.

Jim Tunney, author and former NFL referee, says that many business organizations fail to accomplish what they set out to do because they don't clearly define their target. "If employees don't understand their company's goals and its game plan," he notes, "these goals won't be achieved." He goes on to point out that the game of football never has unclear objectives. "Its goals are always clearly defined," asserts Tunney. "At the end of the field is a goal line. Why do we call it a goal line? Because eleven people on the offensive team huddle for a single purpose—to move the ball across it. Everyone has a specific task to do—the quarterback, the wide receiver, each lineman, every player knows exactly what his assignment is. Even the defensive team has its goal—to prevent the offensive team from achieving its goal."

Pastor, writer, and editor Ed Rowell says, "A dream is a better future in need of an architect who will show others how to make it a reality." If you are a leader, you must be that architect. You must identify the dream and be able to draw it, not only for your benefit but also for the benefit of others.

One night I had dinner in Dallas with an architect named John Fleming. He told me, "If you're an architect, you can't start building a project until you've finished it." By that, he meant that if you're the visionary—the leader—you need to know the end before you start leading the team. You have to see it. If you don't, your team will never be able to fulfill your vision.

As a leader and leadership mentor, I am continually thinking about how to communicate vision to others. If leaders create a fuzzy picture, then people follow in an equally fuzzy way. Lack of clarity hinders initiative, inhibits persistence, and undermines follow-through. Followers don't give their best to something they don't understand. People don't stay on course for something they cannot see. Nobody becomes motivated by something he kinda, sorta believes in.

> *Followers don't give their best to something they don't understand. People don't stay on course for something they cannot see. Nobody becomes motivated by something he kinda, sorta believes in.*

I love the story of how a certain track coach communicated the goal to his runners before a race. Just before the gun sounded, he used to say, "Stay to your left and get back here as soon as you can." It doesn't get any clearer than that!

Anytime a team, department, or organization doesn't see the same clear picture of what it's trying to accomplish, it is destined to get off course. I faced this reality in 1981 when I became the senior pastor of Skyline Wesleyan Church. Although the congregation had experienced growth in the past, it had been stagnant for years. I quickly sensed that the leadership had lost its way. Following my instincts, I asked each member of the board to write the purpose of the church on a three-by-five card. My suspicions were confirmed when I read the cards and found that the seventeen members had written fifteen different answers.

The energy of the church was unfocused, and the direction was unclear. Why? Because the leaders of the organization didn't share a common dream. No wonder they weren't able to move forward. Over the next six months we hammered out our core values and our common vision. As the dream for our church became clearer, the energy of the leadership increased. And the newly focused and energized leaders carried those qualities to the rest of the congregation. The result was that the congregation tripled in size during the next ten years and made a positive impact on the community, which was our dream.

YOU MUST SEE IT TO SEIZE IT

Most people wander through life. They have no clear dream, no clear picture of where they want to go. And even when a great opportunity presents itself to them, they don't have the ability to see it and build a dream upon it.

In 1866 an amateur geologist noticed some South African children playing with a glistening rock. Intrigued, he asked the children's mother if he could purchase it. She said it wasn't worth anything and simply gave it to him. Later when he examined it more closely, his hunch was confirmed: it was a diamond. He calculated its weight at 21 carats.[2]

When others heard of this and other discoveries, a Scottish mineralogist named James Gregory was sent to investigate. He reported that South Africa wasn't suitable for the occurrence of diamonds. He speculated that the previous discoveries had resulted from ostriches, of all things, eating the gems in distant lands and depositing them in South Africa via their dung.

A few days after Gregory's report was made public, an 83 carat diamond was found in the area that he had visited. It is now known as the Star of South Africa, and it launched the region's first mining operation in what is today the world's largest producer of diamonds. And what about Gregory? His name lives on, but not as he might wish. In the diamond industry, when someone exhibits bad judgment, it's called "pulling a Gregory."[3]

Among the people who flocked to South Africa during the diamond rush was Cecil Rhodes, a young man from Britain who dreamed of success. He and his brother saw the potential of diamond mining in the area and bought as many claims as they could. They also purchased an ice-making machine in England, which they brought to Africa so they could sell ice to mine workers suffering in the heat. They used their profits to purchase more mining claims. In the 1880s, Rhodes went on to found De Beers, the largest producer of diamonds in the world.[4]

How would you describe your vision when it comes to your dream? Do you blindly accept the status quo? Or do you look at things with your eyes wide open, seeking greater possibilities? And when you see them, are you serious enough about achieving a dream to actually put it to the test by defining it clearly? Are you willing to describe it in detail, put it on paper, and tell others about it?

Only those who see their dream are able to seize their dream.

If you're not, then you're placing yourself at a disadvantage. Only those who see their dream are able to seize their dream. If you can answer the Clarity Question with a yes because you clearly see your dream, then you are greatly increasing the odds that one day you will do more than just see your dream—you will live it!

It's time to bring clarity to your dream, to give it detail. If you have a general idea of your dream, your temptation may be to start creating your strategy. Don't do it yet. As Mike Hyatt asserted, vision must come first. Begin by writing a detailed description of your dream. Let your imagination go wild. Write as many elements or pieces of it as you can. Don't stop until you have more than you think you need.

Now quantify anything you can. Make it measurable. Don't worry about how you'll get there yet. Be bold. Be audacious. Dream big!

The next step is to state your dream succinctly in writing. Mike broke down his dream into ten clear, measurable elements. Do something similar with your dream. The number doesn't matter—it simply needs to match the dream—but try to keep it fairly short.

Don't expect to be able to do the whole process in one sitting. For most people that's not possible. Instead, give it time. You may want to get away for a retreat to start the process. If you can separate yourself from your usual surroundings or routine for a couple of days, you may be able to get most of the work done. Otherwise, take a day to dream, and then come back to the process for a few hours at a time in subsequent weeks. Don't forget your goal: make your dream as clear and specific as possible. Then keep it in front of you so that you can see it every day.

CHAPTER 3

The Reality Question
Am I Depending on Factors within My Control to Achieve My Dream?

Reality . . . is the enemy of fantasies but not of dreams.

—RUDY RUETTIGER

Dreams, by definition, are not supposed to start with reality. They are supposed to be fantastic, incredible, and out of the box. After all, they are birthed from hopes, desires, and possibilities. They are the products of imagination and creativity. But that also presents a problem. Is a dream worth pursuing if it has *no chance* of becoming reality? I don't think it is.

Many people have been sold a bill of goods when it comes to dreams. They've heard parents, educators, and motivational speakers say things like, "You can go as far as your dreams will take you," and "If you can believe it, you can achieve it." They've read the words of Edmund O'Neil, who asserted of dreamers: "You have the ability to attain whatever you seek; within you is every potential you can imagine. Always aim higher than you believe you can reach. So often, you'll discover you can achieve any goal."

What a crock! I don't believe that about your dreams, and I don't believe that about mine. Yes, we do need to aim high. However, we don't have the ability to attain *whatever* we seek. I don't possess the ability to achieve *every* potential I can imagine. I don't believe that I can achieve *any* goal. That is not reality.

Writer Richard Bach similarly asserts, "You are never given a wish without also being given the power to make it true." If you give that even a moment's rational thought, you know it's not true. At some point in time, just about every child dreams of being able to fly like a bird. Wouldn't that be fantastic? It's not going to happen, no matter how clearly we imagine it.

WRONG SUCCESS MIND-SET

If you have any doubts about the fact that people buy into this false promise, all you have to do is watch the reality TV show *American Idol*. If you've seen the show, you know what I'm talking about. Tens of thousands of people sign up to try out for *American Idol*, but only the very best—and the very worst—get a chance to audition before the judges, who pick competitors for a recording contract.

Some of these contestants are clueless about themselves and their abilities. They sing off key, they screech, they bellow, and they howl. Then they tell everyone how proud and fiercely confident they are about their talent—even the ones who have never sung in public before. And when they are told they aren't good enough by the judges—a professional musician/record producer, a recording artist with six number-one hits, and a record executive (with a combined sixty-plus years of experience)—these wannabe stars throw tantrums, hurl insults, and pronounce, "That's just *your* opinion! I'm great."

I have to admit, I find some of the tryouts entertaining, but I have to wonder where the auditioners' friends and family are. Hasn't anyone ever told them the truth about themselves? Hasn't someone given them a reality check? Everybody except the contestants knows they are totally unqualified to reach their dream!

Believing in a dream isn't enough. Desperately wanting it isn't enough. Are these contestants passionate about their dream? Yes. Are they committed to their dream? Yes, at least in that moment. Are they going to achieve their dream to be the American Idol? No! Why? Because their dream and reality have never met.

TALENT, HARD WORK, AND A DREAM

Contrast that with the story of Andy Hull, the son of John Hull, president and CEO of EQUIP and Injoy Stewardship Services. Andy has always loved music. His mother, Sharon, says that Andy was singing before he learned to talk. And while parents usually have to make their kids practice music, Sharon had to make him *stop* practicing.

Andy got his first guitar when he was eight, and he naturally took to it, teaching himself to play chords. He also picked up and learned to play other instruments, such as the trumpet and piano, but Sharon says he seems to have a special knack for stringed instruments. It came as no surprise when he put together his first band in the sixth grade. He and his friends used to play in a concrete-walled cold room near his house in Toronto. By age thirteen, he and a friend were regularly writing songs together over the phone, using a tape recorder to capture their creations.

When Andy was a junior in high school, he was pretty fed up with school. He was ready to quit, wanting to pursue a career in music. His father's response was, "What's your plan?" Andy gave it some thought and then approached his parents with a proposal: he would leave high school, homeschool himself for his senior year, and make a record during that time. Andy figured he could get his schoolwork done in about two hours a day. That would leave him time to write songs, pull together a band, raise the money he needed for studio time, and record an album. His parents agreed, and he got started. He was right about the schoolwork, and that year he accomplished his goal of recording an album—with the help of a music magazine that gave him some money for studio time.

Though he didn't release that album, the process taught Andy a lot. He solidified the band, which he named Manchester Orchestra, learned about the music business, and came up with a plan for moving forward. Most young musicians are so excited to be signed by a record label that they give their rights away and thus lose control of their music in order to make quick up-front money. The label gives them a large advance, and then the band is expected to work hard to earn the money back. And if the band doesn't give the kind of return the label wants, it drops the band, which is usually never heard from again.

Andy had other ideas. He didn't want to sign a big deal and fall into that trap. Instead, he wanted to release his music online and build a following for his band by touring. He also wanted to create and promote his own record label. He called it Favorite Gentlemen, a name inspired by his favorite players of the Atlanta Braves baseball team.

He turned down several offers from record companies until he found what he considered to be the right fit—a partnership with someone who would sign not only the band but also the Favorite Gentlemen label. Andy finally found that partner in Sony. As part of the deal, he received much less money up front and retained more control of his music. And he received some money from Sony that could be used to sign other bands to his label. Andy's vision was to create a community of artists. One record executive told Andy that he had the best business plan of any nineteen-year-old he'd ever met.

As I write this, Andy is twenty-one years old, is the president of his label, and has signed ten bands, which have released fifteen records so far. Manchester Orchestra has produced and released its first album called *I'm Like a Virgin Losing a Child*. And the band has appeared on *The Late Show with David Letterman* and *Late Night with Conan O'Brien*. In 2007, Manchester Orchestra hit the target of 250 appearances during the year, and in early 2008, the group was preparing to tour the United Kingdom for the fourth time. They were also working on their second album.

Sharon, Andy's mom, says that everything Andy wanted has come to pass, and he's ready to start thinking about his next big dream. I have no doubt that he will be able to reach it.

IF YOU'RE DEPENDING ON LUCK, THEN ALL I CAN SAY IS, "LOTSA LUCK"

I read that Nobel physicist Niels Bohr had a horseshoe nailed to the wall of his office. When a visitor remarked, "Surely a scientist like you doesn't believe in such superstitions," Bohr replied, "Of course not. But I'm told it brings you luck whether you believe in it or not."

> *If your dream depends a lot on luck, then you're in trouble.*
> *If it depends entirely on luck, you're living in Fantasyland.*

If your dream depends a lot on luck, then you're in trouble. If it depends *entirely* on luck, you're living in Fantasyland. Writer of Latin maxims Publius Syrus remarked, "It's a very bad thing to become accustomed to good luck." The worst kind of fantasizers—like the worst *American Idol* auditioners—rely almost entirely on luck to pull off their dreams. They have a lottery mind-set. They believe that if they somehow show up at the right place at the right time with the right number, then presto! Their fantasy will come true.

Wouldn't it be nice if it were that easy? But of course it isn't. Philosopher-poet Ralph Waldo Emerson observed, "Shallow men believe in luck. . . . Strong men believe in cause and effect."

As you move forward in the pursuit of your dream, you need to ask yourself the Reality Question: Am I depending on factors within my control to achieve my dream? People who build their dream on reality take a very different approach to dreams than do people who live in Fantasyland. Take a look at how differently they approach achieving a dream:

FANTASIZERS . . .	DREAM BUILDERS . . .
Rely on luck.	Rely on discipline.
Focus on the destination.	Focus on the journey.

Cultivate unhealthy expectations.	Cultivate healthy discontent.
Minimize the value of work.	Maximize the work they do.
Look for excuses.	Lead to action.
Create inertia.	Generate momentum.
Breed isolation.	Promote teamwork.
Wait.	Initiate.
Avoid personal risks.	Embrace risk as necessary.
Make others responsible.	Make themselves responsible.

> *"Shallow men believe in luck. . . .*
> *Strong men believe in cause and effect."*
> —RALPH WALDO EMERSON

People who are successful in the long run don't leave everything to chance. They focus on what they can do, and then they do it. One of my heroes is John Wooden, the retired highly successful UCLA basketball coach. He is a perfect model of this kind of approach to life. Coach Wooden left nothing to chance. Before he held a practice, he wrote down everything his players would do in detail on three-by-five cards. He started doing that as a coach at South Bend Central College and continued it at Indiana State and UCLA. Why would he go to all that trouble? He didn't want to waste time, and he didn't want to leave the team's success to luck. He wanted to achieve his goals through preparation.

Wooden has stated, "I welcome good luck just as anyone does, but I worked extremely hard to avoid being in a situation in which luck was necessary to produce a favorable outcome or where the luck of an adversary could defeat us. To me, the residue of design—luck—can be important. Much more important, of course, is design."[1] Coach Wooden put it to me another way recently when we met for lunch. "John," he said, "we never took our eye off the basketball and started gazing at the crystal ball." If you want to live your dream, you need to have a similar attitude, focusing on what you can do, not what others, fate, or luck must do for you to succeed.

READ THE FINE PRINT

Columnist Ann Landers wrote, "Rose-colored glasses are never made in bifocals. Nobody wants to read the small print in dreams." What is the fine print when it comes to your dream? The fine print is reality. If you want to achieve your dream, you need to read the proverbial fine print. When you do, here are a few of the things you will find:

The journey will take longer than you hoped.

The obstacles will be more numerous than you believed.

The disappointments will be greater than you expected.

The lows will be lower than you imagined.

The price will be higher than you anticipated.

With all that working against you, it's imperative that you depend on factors within your control to achieve your dream!

Just as anyone who signs a legal contract can't afford to overlook or ignore the fine print, as someone with a dream, you cannot afford to overlook or ignore reality. If you do, the chances are very high that at some point in the pursuit of your dream, reality will stop you cold in your tracks, and you will not be able to take another step forward in your journey.

> "Rose-colored glasses are never made in bifocals. Nobody wants to read the small print in dreams."
>
> —ANN LANDERS

HOW DO YOU RESPOND TO REALITY?

One of the great ironies in life is that you must be acquainted with reality while not allowing your dream to be shattered. Depending on who you are and what your dream is, that can be difficult or easy. Each person is different.

Writer and humorist Sam Levenson reflected on the experience of his parents who had dreamed of coming to America. He stated, "My folks are immigrants and they fell under the spell of the American legend that the streets were paved with gold. When Papa got here he found out three things: 1) The streets were not paved with gold. 2) The streets were not paved at all. 3) He was supposed to do the paving."

For Levenson's parents, reality sank in when they came to America. The good news is that when they were confronted with reality, they didn't try to book a ticket back to their native land. They moved forward, got to work, and made a life for themselves. I hope you will do the same.

Not everyone does. Writer and wit Mark Twain opined, "Get

your facts first, then you can distort 'em as you please." Unfortunately dreams have a way of doing that to many of us. Our desires can be so strong that they distort our picture of reality. That's what happens to many people who audition for *American Idol.* Instead of changing themselves or their dream, they hope reality will change to accommodate them.

The more unrealistic your dream, the more you will be tempted to depend upon things that you cannot control to make it become a reality. The trick is to balance the boldness of dreaming with the reality of your situation. You need to reach far beyond what you think you're capable of but at the same time base what you do on your strengths and other factors within your control. The more concerned you become with things you *can't* control, the less you will do to improve the things you *can* control. And when you do that, you start living in a fantasy world.

> *The more unrealistic your dream, the more you will be tempted to depend upon things that you cannot control to make it become a reality.*

TAKE A LOOK AT YOURSELF

To achieve your dream, you not only need to work hard for it, but you also have to make sure it plays to your strengths. That means knowing what you can and cannot do. When advertising and public relations professor Catherine B. Ahles was vice president for college relations at Macomb Community College, she observed, "We spend most of our twenties discovering all of the hundreds of things we can be. But as we mature into our thirties, we begin to discover all of the things we will never be. The challenge for us as we reach our forties and beyond is to put it all together—to know our capabilities and recognize our limitations—and become the best we can be."[2] It is my hope that this chapter will help you face the reality of your capabilities and limitations, and that they will inform your efforts as you formulate your dream and then put it to the test.

> *The more concerned you become with things you can't control, the less you will do to improve the things you can control.*

IS YOUR DREAM BUILT ON
YOUR REAL STRENGTHS?

The first step in facing reality requires you to look at yourself realistically, to see yourself as you truly are. Nathaniel Branden, a psychiatrist and expert on the subject of self-esteem, has stated that no factor is more decisive in people's psychological development and motivation than the value judgments they make about themselves. He goes on to say that the nature of self-evaluation has a profound effect on a person's values, beliefs, thinking processes, feelings, needs, and goals.

If you've been told you're *capable of anything* you set your mind to—and you've believed it—then you're not being realistic about yourself. On the other hand, if you've been told you'll *never amount*

Focus on my strengths

to anything—and you've believed it—you're not being realistic either. You need to acknowledge where you have no talent or skill *and* see the true potential in your areas of strength. You must be able to put it all together, and you must passionately pursue your dream by building on your strengths. Do you know your strengths? Can you see yourself using those strengths to achieve your dream?

On one of his many American concert tours, the Polish pianist Ignace Paderewski received a visit from an ambitious young woman who told the famous musician that she, too, had enormous musical talent. After much prompting, she persuaded him to let her perform for him. Paderewski then sat through her bumbling, mediocre performance, trying to hide his boredom.

When the young woman had finished playing, she asked, "What do I do now?"

Paderewski sighed and said, "Get married!"

His comment sounds sexist in this day and age, but his point was clear. It didn't matter how much this individual practiced. She was never going to rise to the level of a concert pianist. The skilled Paderewski knew that immediately. When people's talent does not match their dreams and they fail to recognize it, they will be forever working but never winning.

The first step in aligning your dream and your talent is to build on your strengths. That process takes time. I have to admit, it took me about six years early in my career to make adjustments to my focus and start building on my strengths. Through trial and error and the advice of wise people, I eventually turned my attention so that I was facing the right direction to discover my best dreams. And my later success in life can be linked directly to having made this adjustment. I have never known people to be successful while focusing on doing

56

things they hated or were not good at. People who achieve success love what they do and do it well.

> *When people's talent does not match their dreams and they fail to recognize it, they will be forever working but never winning.*

Are you focusing your doing the things you love to do? Are you building on your strengths? Building your dream on your strengths is vitally important. Here's why:

1. Building on Your Strengths Activates the Law of Least Effort

When you build on your strengths, the activities using those strengths come more easily to you. Recently, while reading *You've Got to Read This Book!* I came across the chapter by Farrah Gray, the young entrepreneur and author. He said that when he read about the Law of Least Effort in Deepak Chopra's *The Seven Spiritual Laws of Success*, it had an incredible impact on him. Gray writes,

> The Law of Least Effort is about finding your true purpose and your true area of excellence. I was actually offended when I first read about this law. I said, "He's a fool! I saw my mother work so hard. How dare he say it's not about hard work!" But it was when I followed the Law of Least Effort that my real success began.
>
> The book said that the Law of Least Effort works when you follow your own nature—what is natural for you. If you know and

follow those things, it becomes easy to live your life's purpose. I thought about that and came up with a few questions that helped me figure it out: What comes easy to me but harder to others? What would I want to work on for a long time—even if I was never paid for it? And on the basis of those answers, what could I do to help the people around me?"[3]

Building on strengths obviously worked for Gray. He became a millionaire as a kid-entrepreneur and, at age twenty-two, opened Reality Pros, which manages more than $30 million in assets.[4]

Entertainer Pearl Bailey asserted, "There are two kinds of talent, man-made talent and God-given talent. With man-made talent, you have to work very hard. With God-given talent, you just touch it up once in a while." Which would you rather do? Fight to develop skills where you have little natural gifting, or run with the talent God has already given you and see where it takes you?

> *"There are two kinds of talent, man-made talent and God-given talent. With man-made talent, you have to work very hard. With God-given talent, you just touch it up once in a while."*
>
> —PEARL BAILEY

That's what I've tried to do all of my life. One of the things I'm known for is my public speaking. People continually ask me whether I get nervous when I speak to large audiences—probably because public speaking is at the top of most people's list of fears. When I answer no, people are surprised. When I speak, I am relaxed. It is one of the most enjoyable things I do. I enjoy connecting with people; I am often inspired by new thoughts while on stage. I love to teach and add value to others. Communication is one of my God-given strengths. Trust me, I sweat bullets when I have to do something I'm not good at. If you told me I had to connect a DVD player to your television or change the toner in a copier, forget it. I'm worthless!

When people are going with their strengths and working in their sweet spot, the work they do is simple and easy. However, when they're focusing their effort in an area of weakness, what they do is complex and difficult. To achieve your dream, you have to build on strengths.

2. BUILDING ON YOUR STRENGTHS ENABLES CONSISTENTLY GOOD RESULTS

Dreams don't come true because a person does something well once in a while. Success isn't an event—it's a lifestyle. Dreams are fulfilled when someone performs with excellence day after day. That comes only if you work within an area of strength.

For example, I love golf, but it is not in my strength zone. From time to time, I can hit a great shot. I specifically recall doing that once in 1987! I would be a fool to try to make a living by playing golf. I'd be like the high school home-run hitter who received an invitation to spring training from a major league team. After the first week, he e-mailed home to say, "Dear Mom, leading all batters. These pitchers are not so tough." The next week he boasted, "Now hitting .500 and it looks like I will be starting in the infield." However, the third week, he wrote, "They started throwing curve balls today. Will be home tomorrow."

You cannot achieve success without consistency. You cannot achieve consistency if you are working outside your strengths. It will take all the talent you have to achieve a big dream. Following that talent will give you the greatest chance to be consistently good at what you do.

3. BUILDING ON YOUR STRENGTHS GIVES YOU THE HIGHEST RETURN

Greer Garson, winner of the 1943 Academy Award for best actress, remarked, "Starting out to make money is the greatest mistake in life. Do what you feel you have a flair for doing, and if you are good enough at it, the money will come."

> "Starting out to make money is the greatest mistake in life.
> Do what you feel you have a flair for doing, and if
> you are good enough at it, the money will come."
> —GREER GARSON

Successful people always put their time, energy, and resources into their strengths because they receive the highest return from it. And when they occasionally depart from that approach, as Michael Jordan did when he quit basketball to play baseball, the result is mediocrity. Basketball was Jordan's sweet spot—the thing that would *always* give him the highest return—and most people agree he was one of the best ever to play the game. However, as a baseball player, he lasted one year, never progressed higher than AA ball, batted .202, and finished with 11 fielding errors.[5] That's probably not what he would like to be remembered for.

People can improve a talent only a certain amount. It has been my observation that our potential for growth in a talent area is about 2 points out of 10. In other words, if I am average in an area—let's say a 5—I may be able to become a 6 or 7 by working hard in that area. Occasionally an exceptional person can move up 3 points and become an 8. However, people don't achieve dreams in areas where they are naturally 4s or 5s. If you want to achieve a dream, you need to work in an area where you start as a 7 or 8. Then if you work hard, you can be truly exceptional!

Here is what I know: you have some wonderful strengths that make you unique and hold great possibilities for your future. You just have to find them. I once saw a sign in a hardware store that stated, "We've got it if you can find it." That sign could be applied to your life. You've got it, but you have to find it.

IS YOUR DREAM BUILT ON YOUR REAL HABITS?

In answering the Reality Question, you need to start by building on your strengths. However, that is just the start. J. Paul Getty, philanthropist and founder of the Getty Oil Company, explained, "The individual who wants to reach the top in business must appreciate the might and force of habit. He must be quick to break those habits that can break him—and hasten to adopt those practices that will become the habits that help him achieve the success he desires." That observation is true not just in business but in every endeavor. A dream becomes reality as a result of your actions, and your actions are controlled, to a large extent, by your habits.

I once read that psychologists estimate that up to 90 percent of people's behavior is habitual—90 percent! Most of the things you do are governed by routine. Think about how you started your days this week. You probably showered, dressed, ate, and drove to work using the same pattern you do every day. If you're like most people, you didn't expend any energy thinking about how you would do these things; you just did them. You start your workday, clean your house, shop for groceries, and read the newspaper pretty much the same way. You have a routine, a set of habits. Your habits impact every aspect of your life, from health to wealth to relationships.

The good news is that habits can help us do things more quickly and remove mental clutter so that we can think about more important things. The bad news is that they can also be detrimental to our health or lead us in a direction different from that of our dreams. Think about the person who dreams of winning marathon races but smokes two packs of cigarettes a day. Or the person who dreams of being a fashion model but eats six thousand calories a day without exercising. Or the businessperson who dreams of leading a winning team but habitually insults and belittles employees.

The Greek philosopher Aristotle observed, "We are what we repeatedly do. Excellence then is not an act, but a habit." Your daily habits will determine the outcome of your life. The secret to your success can be found in your daily agenda. Successful people don't just drift to victory. Individuals who achieve big dreams don't get there by accident. The longer you practice good habits in a positive, disciplined, and focused way, the greater the chance your future will be positive. The longer you practice bad habits, the greater the chance it will be negative.

> *"We are what we repeatedly do.*
> *Excellence then is not an act, but a habit."*
>
> —ARISTOTLE

The older I get, the more I have seen this come into play in people's lives. Habits have a cumulative effect—but the results don't usually show up until much later in life. If the habits are bad, by the time the damage is evident, it's often too late to alter the results. That's why you need to take control of your habits at your earliest opportunity!

Speaker and author Robert Ringer, in *Million Dollar Habits,* expounds on the power of positive habits. "The world is saturated with intelligent, highly educated, extraordinarily skilled people," writes Ringer, "who experience ongoing frustration because of their lack of success. Millions of others spend their lives working hard, long hours only to die broke." His solution? Cultivate the right habits and practice them regularly. Says Ringer,

> Remember, life is nothing more than the sum total of many successful years; a successful year is nothing more than the sum total of many successful months; a successful month is nothing more than the sum total of many successful weeks; a successful week is nothing more than the sum total of many successful days. That's why practicing successful habits day in and day out is the most certain way to win over the long term.[6]

Habits are important in achieving your dream. They are taking you in a particular direction. And you have to take a realistic look at yourself to know where your habits are taking you. If <u>your habits</u> <u>don't line up with your dream, then you need to either change your</u> <u>habits or change your dream.</u> If you want to hold on to your dream, then be prepared for a battle to change your habits because a bad habit never goes away by itself.

> *If your habits don't line up with your dream, then you need to either change your habits or change your dream.*

It's uncomfortable, and it can feel unnatural to do something different from what you've always done. As an example of what I mean, try these short activities:

- Put your hands together and interlace your fingers. When people do this, they *always* put the same thumb on top. Now, separate your hands and interlace your fingers again, but do it so that your other thumb is in the top position. Doesn't it feel odd?
- Cross your arms. Once again, when people do this, they always put the same arm on top. Uncross and recross them, putting the other arm on top.
- Clap your hands. You naturally favor one hand as the main clapper and the other as the receiver. Now try switching them.

If someone asked you from now on to do those three things in the opposite way from the way you typically do them, it would feel awkward and uncomfortable. It would also take continual effort on your part to change. That's how you will feel as you work to change the habits in your life. But you have to be willing to make such changes. Won't the effort be worth it if you know that down the road your new habits are going to get you closer to your dream? Think of it as your very own undo-it-yourself project.

IS YOUR DREAM BUILT ON YOUR REAL POTENTIAL?

Finally, you need to build your strengths on your real potential. In life, you can't change where you are starting from. You are where you are—that's a fact. The best you can do is to work hard to change where you end up. If you want to end up in a place where you are achieving your dream, you will have to make sure you have aligned your strengths, your habits, and your potential. If they don't line up in the same direction—toward your dream—then you're in trouble.

Today my strengths seem pretty obvious to me and to others. I am good at leading, communicating, creating, and networking. I can do only those four with excellence. At all other things, I'm average or worse. My weaknesses abound and are obvious to me and those around me. To compensate, I have developed a team of people who complement my weaknesses, and I have created systems and habits to help me build on my strengths. Here are the critical habits I practice to move me closer to my dream:

- Every day I read on the subject of leadership.
- Every day I file on the subject of leadership.
- Every day I write on the subject of leadership.
- Every day I talk about the subject of leadership.

- Every day I ask questions about the subject of leadership.
- Every day I train people on the subject of leadership.
- Every day I think on the subject of leadership.
- Every day I add value to people on the subject of leadership.
- Every day I talk to leaders on the subject of leadership.
- Every day I try to cultivate good relationships with leaders.
- Every day I work to gain the respect of leaders.
- Every day I try to add value to leaders without expecting something in return.

Although I do these things every day, I don't have a lot to show for it in a few days, weeks, or months. But I have a great deal to show for it after several years. And after several decades, it *really* begins to compound. Why do I go to so much effort? Because my dream is to add value to leaders who multiply value to others. My current situation, my strengths, my habits, and my potential all line up.

It is impossible for me to tell you the habits that you need to develop to make your dream come true because I do not know your dream, nor do I know the potential that God has put in you. But here is what I know: if you know your strengths and build on them by doing what is needed to make your dream a reality, and you do them consistently until they become habits, the odds are very high that you can achieve your dream. For most people, the limitations they face aren't on the outside, only on the inside.

> *For most people, the limitations they face aren't on the outside, only on the inside.*

MAKE REALITY YOUR ALLY

He wanted to be a conductor. However, his style was odd, to say the least. When conducting soft passages, he'd crouch down. When the music called for a crescendo, he'd leap into the air with a shout. One time he jumped to cue a dramatic passage, but the musicians didn't respond. He'd lost track of his place and jumped too soon. The musicians often looked to the first violinist instead of him for direction.

Beethoven

His memory was not very good. During a performance, he tried to conduct the orchestra through a section of music he had instructed them to skip. When they didn't play the passage, he stopped conducting altogether and shouted, "Stop! Wrong! That will not do! Again! Again!"

He had a clumsiness about him. When he conducted for a piano concerto he had written, he tried to do it from the piano while playing and knocked candles off the piano. During another concert, he knocked over one of the choir boys.

The musicians begged him to give up his dream of becoming a great conductor. Finally he did. From then on, Ludwig van Beethoven gave up conducting and focused his attention on composing.

How are you doing when it comes to the Reality Question? Are you trying to do something that you're really not suited for? Have you aligned your abilities, habits, potential, and aspirations so that you have a great probability for success? Or are you depending on luck or other people to achieve your dreams? If so, it's time to make adjustments.

Reality is never the enemy of a dream—as long as you can positively answer the Reality Question: Am I depending on factors within my control to achieve my dream?

Check to make sure that your personal alignment is right for you to achieve your dream. Answer each of the following questions:

1. **What is my dream?** If you haven't already written out your dream, do so now.

2. **What is my starting point?** Define where you are now. You may have already described this if you followed the instructions at the end of the previous chapter.

3. **What are my strengths and weaknesses?** Describe your top three to five abilities. Any dream you desire to reach will have to build on these strengths. If it helps you, draw a circle around the top three to five things. Anything that is not written in that circle is a weakness! You can build upon only these few strengths to achieve your dream. Anything else will require you to depend on factors outside your control. Make adjustments to your dream accordingly.

4. **What are my current positive and negative habits?** Make three columns. In the first, write all of your current habits that appear to contribute positively to your dream. In the second, write all of the current habits that undermine your progress. In the third, write the new habits you will need to cultivate to progress toward your dream. If you are unsure about this step, sit down with a trusted mentor who knows you well or another person with experience in your area of interest and get his advice.

5. **How long must I practice these habits to reach my potential?** Estimate how much work it will take for you to develop into the person who can achieve his or her dream. Verify your assessment with a trusted mentor or adviser.

CHAPTER 4

The Passion Question
Does My Dream Compel Me to Follow It?

If you are working on something exciting that you really care about, you don't have to be pushed. The vision pulls you.

—STEVE JOBS

Have you ever gone to a carnival or game arcade and seen one of the machines called the passion meter? It's supposed to be able to measure how romantic you are. It usually has a panel of flashing lights and a metal handle that you squeeze while a mild electrical current flows through it. The longer and stronger you can squeeze the handle, the better your score.

Wouldn't it be nice if the passion for our dreams could be as easily measured? Just drop a quarter into the machine, give the handle a squeeze, and it predicts the odds for our success! But real life isn't like that. The Passion Question, which asks, Does my dream compel me to follow it? can be a difficult one to answer. How can you know whether your passion will be enough to carry you through to the realization of your dream?

passion is the starting point for all achievement

PASSION CREATES POSSIBILITY

Passion is a critical element for anyone who wants to achieve a dream. Why? Because it is the starting point of all achievement. I have never seen anyone anywhere at any time achieve anything of any value without the spark of passionate desire! It provides the energy that makes dreams possible. "Then why," you may be asking, "didn't you make it the subject of the first chapter of this book?" I'll tell you: because too many people say that passion is the end-all and be-all of dreams, but that isn't true. Passion alone will not be enough for you to achieve your dream. The Passion Question is only one of ten that you must be able to answer affirmatively to succeed. On the other hand, if you *cannot* answer it affirmatively, you may run out of steam before you reach your dream.

> *Passion is a critical element for anyone*
> *who wants to achieve a dream. Why? Because*
> *it is the starting point of all achievement.*

The road to any dream is cluttered with detours, problems, and disappointments. Unfortunately, many people have so much difficulty on that road that their dreams die there. That's why passion is so important. It keeps the dream alive, even during tough times. It inspires you. It's why Danish philosopher Søren Kierkegaard stated, "If I were to wish for anything, I should not wish for wealth and power, but for the passionate sense of potential, for the eye which sees the potential. Pleasure disappoints; possibility never."

THE POWER OF PASSION

What is passion? It's an enthusiasm that not only gives you energy and focus in the present, but also gives you power to keep moving toward the future. It gives you fuel to pursue your dream. To paraphrase columnist Will Hobbs, passion makes possible waking up in the morning, whoever you are, wherever you are, however old or young, and bounding out of bed because there's something out there that you love to do, that you believe in, that you're good at—something that's bigger than you are, and you can hardly wait to get at it again today.

If I had to put it into the simplest possible terms, I would say that passion does three significant things for us:

1. PASSION PULLS US UP—ENABLING US TO OVERCOME ADVERSITY

Anytime you try to accomplish something of value, you will face adversity. Passion can help you get through it. In July 2007 I spoke for Maxima Global Consulting in Johannesburg, South Africa. Though the trip to Johannesburg was long, I found the conference to be a very enjoyable experience. The day after the event, I had the opportunity to sit down with the organizers and talk to them about it. Thalita Boikhutso, the company's group chief executive and a ten-year veteran in people development, had been responsible for putting the event together. As we talked, she kept saying it was "a dream come true." When I asked her to explain, she said that the previous year, she had come up with a new leadership development concept for the company: an international leadership event.

"I made a decision in 2006," she said, "that each year I will do at least one big thing that would grow not only me, but many other people in my country. What was my definition of *big*? For me it was something I believed was impossible, something high risk. Dr. Maxwell, bringing you to South Africa for this event was my big thing for 2007, and I was determined to make it happen."

She went on to describe the many obstacles she had to overcome to hold the conference, such as not winning over her business partner until she pledged to reimburse the company out of her own pocket for any losses. When she failed to enlist other corporate sponsors, she didn't give up. Her passion carried her through and won over her team.

"Before the conference, many knew what the event meant for me and our business," Thalita said, "but very few comprehended what it meant for them and their organizations. At the end of the conference, many wished they had invited friends, families, and more people from their organizations; many wished the conference could run for another day; many wished they could have a similar conference in the near future; and many summed up their overall experience of the conference in one word: *magnifique*. The journey was long, but the benefits at the end of it all—priceless. And that was a dream come true for me!"

The most inspirational part of any dream is its beginning. We've all experienced the thrill of birthing a dream. We see the possibilities. We feel the excitement of what could be. We envision a positive future. We may enjoy the affirmation of friends who want us to succeed. And then . . . we begin. We quickly realize that between the dream's inspiration and its manifestation, there's going to be lot of perspiration! As every new parent finds out, it's much harder having and raising the baby than making it.

> *Between the dream's inspiration and its manifestation, there's going to be lot of perspiration!*

What carries you through the tough times? What gives you the power to overcome adversity? Passion! Poet William Arthur Ward suggested that the key to success is to

Believe while others are doubting.
Plan while others are playing.
Study while others are sleeping.
Decide while others are delaying.
Prepare while others are daydreaming.
Begin while others are procrastinating.
Work while others are wishing.
Save while others are wasting.
Listen while others are talking.
Smile while others are frowning.
Commend while others are criticizing.
Persist while others are quitting.[1]

What will give you the energy to believe, plan, study, decide, prepare, begin, work, save, listen, smile, commend, and persist? The answer is passion!

2. PASSION PUSHES US OUT—GIVING US INITIATIVE

To succeed in life, we must stay within our strength zone but continually move outside our comfort zone. Think about it. Have you ever accomplished anything of significance while you were in your comfort zone? I bet the answer is no.

> *To succeed in life, we must stay within our strength zone*
> *but continually move outside our comfort zone.*

Most of us do not like moving outside our comfort zone. We resist it. We like to feel safe and secure. We don't want to look foolish or to fall flat on our faces. And as we get older, we tend naturally to become more and more complacent. That's a problem because complacency kills passion. It reduces us to average. It clips our wings and keeps us from soaring, no matter how much we want to. It puts our dreams beyond our reach.

It takes initiative to be successful, to achieve a dream. It requires us to take risks. Playwright George Bernard Shaw asserted, "I'm sick of all the reasonable people: they see all the reasons for doing nothing." Passion makes us unreasonable. It prompts us to leave our comfort zone and cross the threshold of our doubt. It pushes us out the door so that we can get going on the journey toward our dreams.

3. Passion Positions Us Well—Giving Us the Greatest Odds for Success

Missionary doctor Albert Schweitzer observed, "Success is not the key to happiness. Happiness is the key to success. If you love what you are doing, you will be successful." When we have passion and we allow ourselves to pursue it, it positions us well in life. It sets us up for success. If we don't follow our passion, we will be in a difficult place, one that will not serve us well. As Richard Elder advised:

Safe living generally makes for regrets later on. We are all given talents and dreams. Sometimes the two don't match. But more often than not, we compromise both before ever finding out. Later on, as successful as we might be, we find ourselves looking back longingly to that time when we should have chased our true dreams and our true talents for all they were worth. Don't let yourself be pressured into thinking that your dreams or your talents aren't prudent. They were never meant to be prudent. They were meant to bring joy and fulfillment into your life.[2]

> *"Success is not the key to happiness.*
> *Happiness is the key to success. If you love what*
> *you are doing, you will be successful."*
> —ALBERT SCHWEITZER

The majority of people in the world don't follow their passion. As a result, they are frustrated and unhappy. And you can see that in how they live their lives. Publisher Malcolm Forbes affirmed, "The biggest mistake people make in life is not trying to make a living at what they enjoy." As a result, they simply try to endure their working lives instead of making the most of them. They live for the weekends. They try to hang on until retirement. That's really a shame because people's chances of success are directly proportional to the degree of pleasure they derive from what they do. When they settle, they put themselves in a tough place. When they follow their passion, they position themselves well.

Tommy Lasorda, the retired manager of the Los Angeles Dodgers, displayed his passion for baseball during a radio interview after his team suffered a demoralizing defeat in the National League playoffs. Despite the loss, he still talked enthusiastically about the game. The host was amazed and asked him how he could be so upbeat after losing such an important game.

"The best day of my life is when I manage a winning game," Lasorda responded. "And the second best day of my life is when I manage a losing game." The seasoned manager's passion was baseball, and every day he was involved in the game was a day he was living his dream.

Dreams come true when gifts are set on fire with passion. The best career advice you will ever receive is to discover your passion and follow it. When you make your dream your profession, you experience fulfillment most of the days of your life. Author Logan Pearsall Smith observed, "There are two things to aim at in life; first, to get what you want; and after that, to enjoy it. Only the wisest of mankind achieve the second."[3]

> *"There are two things to aim at in life; first,*
> *to get what you want; and after that, to enjoy it.*
> *Only the wisest of mankind achieve the second."*
> —LOGAN PEARSALL SMITH

GUITAR MAN

One person who has gotten what he wants and certainly enjoys it is Bob Taylor. I met Bob in the early 1980s when I was the leader of Skyline Church in San Diego. Bob played guitar on the worship team. My first impression of him was that he was a really nice guy. He was sharp, but also pretty laid-back—except when he talked about one subject: guitars. You see, Bob is the founder and president of Taylor Guitars, and making guitars is his life's work and consuming passion.

Since he was a kid, Bob has been captivated by two interests. The first is knowing how things work. He says that when he was young, "playing" with his toys always involved a screwdriver and a wrench. Whatever he got on Christmas Day was inevitably deconstructed by December 26.

"To me," says Bob, "an electric train was fun only if it taught you something about how electric motors worked. I didn't see the point of just watching the train go round and round."

Bob's other interest was guitars. He bought his first acoustic guitar from a friend for three dollars when he was nine. It wasn't long before he began tinkering with it. When he was ten, he sawed off the neck and tried to use it to create an electric guitar. It didn't work, but even at that age he was willing to try building just about anything.

In junior high and high school, Bob was a shop class wizard and won the California State Industrial Arts Exposition two years in a row with metal shop projects. But when he was in eleventh grade, he switched over to wood shop and set his sights on a project even his teacher couldn't complete: a twelve-string guitar. It took him most of the year, but he built one.

The next year Bob built two more guitars in his spare time. After that, he knew what he wanted to do with his life. He promptly told his parents that he wasn't going to college but would instead become a guitar builder. His mother cried. She feared that he wouldn't be successful. But people don't need to follow the common path to be successful. They need to follow their passion.

In September 1973, just three months after graduating from high school, Bob was working at a bench in a little independent hippie guitar-making shop called the American Dream where each worker functioned as a semi-independent contractor. Bob immediately made an impression. Another guitar maker who worked there says of Bob, "He came in out of high school and he just blew everybody [away] with the speed and quality of his work. All he did was put his head down and go. . . . He just had a drive to excel that was unlike anything I'd ever seen."[4]

Bob got to work using some of the shop owner's tools and other ones he had designed and made in high school metal shop. He gained knowledge, speed, and experience as he worked.

"It took me a month to build that first guitar," recalls Bob, "which was really far too long. I was only making a couple of hundred dollars on each guitar, and I couldn't make a living if I was only building twelve guitars a year. At that time, my body and mind were the tools that I viewed as needing the most improvement, so I worked on my skills and attitude. I began to learn how to make guitars faster and better with my own bare hands. Later in my career I began to use tooling to speed up the construction process."[5]

Bob worked hard and kept experimenting with new building techniques. His hunger to build great guitars grew with every project.

He found the whole thing very compelling: "There is no feeling quite like selling a guitar that you made yourself."[6]

FROM GUITAR BUILDER TO BUSINESS OWNER

About a year after Bob arrived, the shop's owner, who never made any money, decided to sell it. Two young men who worked there refinishing guitars decided to make an offer. One of them, Kurt Listug, was advised by his father to add someone who actually knew how to build guitars as a third partner. Bob was already the best in the shop, so Kurt asked him to join them. In October 1974 the three of them bought the shop and opened for business. Because Bob was the guitar maker, they decided to put the name Taylor on the instruments.

During the next year or so, they all worked hard. Bob was the main builder and designer. He bought logs to be sawed for guitar wood. He developed new building techniques and designs, such as a bolt-on neck. He even designed and built his tools when needed. And he talked to every guitar maker and repair person he could find. He was constantly trying to learn.

Meanwhile, Kurt Listug tried to run the business while also helping out in the shop. But it was a struggle, especially financially. For ten years they limped along, several times taking on loans to keep things going. In the early years, they didn't pay themselves anything. It was a big deal to Bob in 1977 when the partners finally decided to pay themselves a salary of fifteen dollars a week. Unfortunately, their paychecks often went uncashed because they knew there wasn't enough money in the bank to cover them. In 1983, Bob and Kurt bought out the third partner who no longer shared their enthusiasm for the business.

Despite the horrible financial difficulties, Bob loved it. When he was at the shop, he was building guitars. When he wasn't, he was thinking about it. "I was stressed out about the lack of money," Bob explains. "But I was actually pretty happy during the day because I was actually building guitars and living my dream. Really the only reason that guitars needed to be sold, for my purposes, was so that I could keep making them. . . . I was just afraid that we'd go out of business and I'd have to get a job doing something I hated."[7]

THE PASSION FINALLY PAYS OFF FINANCIALLY

In the mid-1980s, things started to turn around, despite acoustic guitars being out of fashion in the music scene. Production of guitars at the company was up to twenty-two a week. And Kurt Listug was succeeding in getting music stores to buy guitars. For the first time, they were actually making a profit. What carried them through was their passion! It continually fueled their dreams. Says finger-picking-style guitar champion Chris Proctor, "Bob wakes up in the morning and wants to make the guitars better. Kurt wakes up and wants to make the company better."[8]

Today Taylor Guitars is one of the most successful instrument makers in the world. The company is known for innovation in the design and construction of instruments. Using Bob's passion, incredible knowledge of guitars, and ability to design and build tools, the company has pioneered the use of computer-controlled milling machines, created environmentally friendly finishes, and developed building techniques that aid in the conservation of increasingly limited supplies of exotic wood. All the while, the employees have produced guitars of excellent craftsmanship and incredible consistency. And the company has grown incredibly. Today Taylor employs more than 450 people and produces more than seventy-two thousand instruments a year.[9]

What's even more remarkable is that Taylor Guitars is also known for sharing its expertise with other manufacturers. Why? Bob loves guitars and the people who make them. He remembers how open and helpful other guitar makers were in the early days when he was just learning.

"Since then I've felt that I should be as free with my knowledge as those builders were with theirs," he says.[10] "I think I'd be content to know that after I've gone, people said, 'He left the world of guitars better off than when he found it.' I think that would be a good way to be remembered."[11]

READING THE PASSION METER

So how passionate are you about your dream? Do you wake up in the morning and go to bed at night thinking about your dream the way Bob does? Are you willing to pursue it even if you can't make a living at it? Are you willing to plug away at it, improving your skills and attitude for more than a decade before others recognize you for it? Even now, as perhaps the most successful guitar maker in the world, Bob Taylor is still trying to figure out new ways to make a better guitar. He is relentless. In recent years, the company that had always built acoustics has begun to manufacture innovative electric guitars. And what's really remarkable is that even with his passion and focus, Bob is a strong family man who has been married more than thirty years!

People who achieve their dream answer yes to the Passion Question. They feel *compelled* to follow their dream. They don't care whether it seems normal or practical. Even when he was in high school, as Bob worked on his first guitar people thought he was weird and tried to discourage him.

"Hey, Taylor, what are you building?" they'd ask.

"A guitar," he'd answer.

"You are not. He thinks he's building a guitar, but he's not. He'll never get it done," they'd chide.

"Okay, I'm not," Bob would answer and keep right on working. "It was pretty weird but it didn't bother me much because I was used to being a dork and doing stuff on my own," says Bob.[12]

How do you gauge your passion? Going back to the idea of the passion meter, how would you score when it comes to your dream? Look at the scale below that could be used to gauge a person's attitude toward any given subject:

PASSION SCALE

10. My passion is so hot that it sets other people on fire.
9. I cannot imagine my life without my dream.
8. I willingly sacrifice other important things for it.
7. I am fired up by it and often preoccupied with it.
6. I enjoy it as one of many interests.
5. I can take it or leave it.
4. I prefer not to think about it.
3. I go out of my way to avoid it.
2. I've put it on my list of least favorite things.
1. I would rather have a root canal without anesthesia.

Trying to gauge Bob Taylor's passion for guitars, I recognize that he scores a 10. I'm not a musician, but when Bob talks about guitars, he even gets *me* excited. His passion is compelling.

What is my passion? Adding value to leaders. I think about it all the time. I've made sacrifices in many other areas of my life to learn about leadership. I have focused the last twenty years of my life on it. And when I talk about it, other people get fired up too. It's what I love and live for. When I teach leadership, I can't help but think, *I was made for this!*

Think about your dream. Now take another look at the Passion Scale. Which entry best describes you? If you score lower than an 8, your dream might be in trouble. A willingness to sacrifice is merely the *entry point* for having enough passion to achieve a dream. Anything less, and it might not be enough to keep you going. And that brings up another important aspect of passion: staying power. Being on fire about your dream won't be enough if you can't keep that fire going. If you're like most people, you will have to follow your passion a long time before you receive any external reward for it.

> *If you're like most people, you will have to follow your passion a long time before you receive any external reward for it.*

STOKING THE FIRE

If your passion level is an 8, 9, or 10, you're in good shape. But what if it's not? Does that mean you're doomed? If you don't feel highly compelled to follow your dream, will you never see it come to fruition? Not necessarily. There is, of course, a chance that you are not embracing the right dream and you need to revisit the Ownership and Reality Questions. However, you can be on the right track and still not have enough fuel for the trip. If that's where you find yourself, know that you can do specific things to stoke the fire of your passion. Try these things that can give you more energy to move forward:

1. TAKE INTO ACCOUNT YOUR NATURAL TEMPERAMENT

Everybody isn't the same. Perhaps your natural personality type is melancholic (you like things done right) or phlegmatic (you value peacefulness); you may not be a naturally enthusiastic or demonstrative person. That's okay. You just need to take that into account. My writer, Charlie Wetzel, possesses both of these personality traits. As a result, he's not the type of person who hoots and hollers and gets all excited about the things he cares about. However, he makes up for that with sheer perseverance. He has worked on more than forty-five books with me in the last fourteen years. Nobody does that without staying power. And if you're like Charlie, you can probably tap into the stubborn sustainability that comes along with his personality type.

Conversely, perhaps your personality is sanguine (you like things fun) or choleric (you want things done your way); you're likely to be highly passionate about *anything* you care about. However, you are also likely to lose interest in things rather quickly. Your heat is very high but doesn't last. That is my personality profile. I become very excited about something, but I like to quickly move on to the next big thing. You need to take that into account too.

Here's the bottom line: sustaining your passion is like cooking.

One piece of beef, like a filet, cooks best at very high heat for a short time. Another, like chuck, cooks best at a lower heat for a longer time. Either way, you can have a delicious meal. You just need to know what kind of meat you have and how to cook it.

2. KEEP YOUR EYE ON WHAT'S IMPORTANT TO YOU

In one of the best leadership books I've ever read, *The Leadership Challenge* by James Kouzes and Barry Posner, the authors asked John H. Stanford, who was a major general in the U.S. Army, how he developed leaders. Stanford replied:

> When anyone asks me that question, I tell them I have the secret to success in life. The secret to success is to stay in love. Staying in love gives you the fire to ignite other people, to see inside other people, to have a greater desire to get things done than other people. A person who is not in love doesn't really feel the kind of excitement that helps them to get ahead and to lead others to achieve. I don't know any other fire, any other thing in life that is more exhilarating and is more positive a feeling than love is.[13]

Stanford realized that he had to keep his passion—love for people—in the forefront or he would not be able to lead them well. Many people don't do that. They lose sight of what really matters for them, and as a result, their fire goes out.

If you're not feeling passionate about your dream, remember what's important to you and why you wanted to pursue your dream in the first place. As long as you keep that in mind, it will be easier for you to keep the fire burning.

3. Overcome the Fear of Being Different
   from Others

I already mentioned that Bob Taylor was different from his peers. The kids in his high school often didn't understand him. But you may be surprised to know that when he went to work at the American Dream guitar shop at age nineteen, he didn't really fit in there either. Greg Deering, who already worked there when Bob arrived, recalls, "Bob was different from everyone else there. He was the only person, apart from me and Sam [the owner], who wasn't a long-haired hippie."[14] Bob didn't care that he was different. He followed his dream anyway.

Early in my career, I felt like an outsider. I never felt that I fit in with the other people I knew in ministry. I never was "one of the boys." In the beginning, that bothered me. But I believed in what I was doing, and I wanted to build a church that would make an impact. I forged ahead. It took many years, but eventually I was able to do it. And then to my surprise, people started coming to me to seek advice.

People who achieve their dreams stand out. You cannot be part of the crowd and achieve your dream at the same time. If you want to live an extraordinary life and do extraordinary things, you need to follow your passion and not worry about what others think of you.

> *People who achieve their dreams stand out.*
> *You cannot be part of the crowd and*
> *achieve your dream at the same time.*

4. Resist the Apathy That Often Accompanies Aging

Children are naturally passionate and enthusiastic. They love life and dream big. Some retain that enthusiasm and energy through childhood and into early adulthood. But somewhere along the line, most human beings lose their enthusiasm for life and become more and more apathetic. Perhaps that occurs because they lose their idealism. Or maybe conflict and day-to-day difficulties discourage them. Either way, they lose their passion. Many settle into comfortable but unrewarding routines, and they give up.

Don't allow that to happen to you. No matter what disappointments or difficulties you've faced, don't let them sap your passion. Even people who have had to deal with tragedies are able to find purpose in them. At every age and stage of life, there are obstacles and advantages, trials and triumphs. It's up to you to make the most of the positive and not let the negative get you down. For example, now that I've passed age sixty, I've found that my energy is much lower than it used to be. That bothered me a lot at first because I didn't want to slow down. But now I make the most of my leisure time and enjoy more time with my family, including my five grandchildren. I'm enjoying this time of my life more than any other.

So how do you answer the Passion Question? Does your dream compel you to follow it? If not, are you willing to do what it takes to increase your passion to a level that will carry you over obstacles and sustain you for the long haul?

Passion alone will not be enough to make your dream a reality. But I can think of few things that are more important than passion. Doing what you love and loving what you do continually provide fuel that can keep you going. They can transform the way you think, the way you work, and the way you interact with others. Passion has the power to transform you. As author and critic John Ruskin observed, "When love and skill work together, expect a masterpiece." Isn't that what you would like your life to be?

> *"When love and skill work together, expect a masterpiece."*
> —JOHN RUSKIN

CAN YOU ANSWER YES TO THE PASSION QUESTION: DOES MY DREAM COMPEL ME TO FOLLOW IT?

If you lack passion for the pursuit of your dream, you must resolve the issue to be successful in that area of your life:

- *Do you lack passion because you do not own your dream?* If so, set aside time for reflection and self-examination to revisit the Ownership Question and determine whether your dream is really *your* dream.

- *Do you lack passion because you do not see it clearly enough?* If this is a problem, imagine a clear picture of your dream, and then capture it in writing.

- *Do you lack passion because your dream doesn't match your talent and skills?* It's hard to remain passionate about something you cannot succeed in doing. Confirm that your dream is based on your gifting and on factors within your control.

- *Does your natural temperament disguise your passion?* If you are the type of person who doesn't get excited easily, then try to tap into your sense of purpose to keep you focused and harness your natural staying power, keeping whatever passion you have burning.

- *Is your passion stifled by a fear of being different?* If you are worried about being different, read biographies of people you admire who have fulfilled their dreams in areas similar to yours. You may find inspiration in knowing that you are similar to your heroes.

❄ *Has your passion been diminished as you have gotten older?* If aging has threatened to put out the spark you once had for your dream, you need to discern whether the dream was a product of a different season of life or whether it is something that continues to be worthy of your time and energy. Think about why you were interested in the first place. Remembering your original inspiration may fire you up again. If not, it may be time to modify your dream according to your current season of life.

Every person is capable of discovering and harnessing the power of passion—no matter what age, stage of life, or temperament. It's never too early or too late to dream.

CHAPTER 5

The Pathway Question
Do I Have a Strategy to Reach My Dream?

We must look for ways to be an active force in our lives.
We must take charge of our own destinies, design a life
of substance, and truly begin to live our dreams.

—LES BROWN

Several months ago after attending an NFL game, I went to dinner with a group of friends. Most of them were in their thirties and I, at age sixty, was the elder statesman of the group. So I decided to ask them questions about their views on football, politics, and their dreams. One question I asked was, "If you could do one thing to change the world, what would it be?" Some had never considered the idea before and had difficulty answering. Others expressed involved and lofty goals.

"So what would you do, John?" one person asked after many had shared their responses. It was something I've thought about. My answer was that I'd teach every child in the world to read. I believe the ability to read can open the door to all other learning and personal growth.

DREAMING OF POTENTIAL

Recently I read an article about someone who has also been thinking about changing the world by helping children learn. And to his credit, he is doing more than just dreaming about it; he is working hard to make it a reality. His name is Nicholas Negroponte. He started his career studying architecture at MIT, focusing on the groundbreaking field of computer-aided design. After receiving his bachelor's and master's degrees, he joined MIT's faculty in 1966. Since then, he has been involved in innovative projects using computers.[1]

I have to admit that I'm not a technology guy. When I sit down to write, I use a pen and legal pad. However, I came across an article that intrigued me. It was about a $150 laptop computer called the XO that was being created to help children in developing countries to learn. It was the brainchild of Nicholas Negroponte.

In 1982, Negroponte accepted the French government's invitation to be part of an experimental project using computers in developing countries.[2] With some computers donated by Steve Jobs, Negroponte and others worked with children in Senegal. The project met with limited success, but the experience planted the original seed for what eventually became One Laptop Per Child (OLPC)—an initiative to create low-cost computers for children in developing nations around the world, even in places where there was no running water, electricity, or telephone service.

Negroponte dreamed of creating a device that would be innovative and rugged, yet simple. It would have few moving parts and be able to take a pounding in hostile environments. It would automatically network itself to other computers of the same kind and use little energy. (It could even be run using solar or hand-cranked power.)

And all the software on it would be open source, meaning that it wouldn't be protected by copyright and could be used, accessed, and modified by anyone and everyone. The concept became known as the "$100 laptop."

With his forty years of experience in innovation, Negroponte had the ability and connections to facilitate the creation of such a device. But the technology wasn't what captivated him. Rather, it was the people it would help. As he often told people, "OLPC is a learning project, not a laptop project." Negroponte's perspective is captured by OLPC's mission statement: "Any nation's most precious natural resource is its children. We believe the emerging world must leverage this resource by tapping into the children's innate capacities to learn, share, and create on their own. Our answer to that challenge is the XO laptop, a children's machine designed for 'learning learning.'"[3]

In 2006, Negroponte stepped down from his position as chairman of MIT's Media Lab so that he could devote the rest of his life to the fulfillment of his dream of seeing children grow and fulfill their potential.

FINDING A PATHWAY TO SUCCESS

Some people were quick to criticize Negroponte's dream. Intel's chairman Craig Barrett remarked, "Mr. Negroponte has called it a $100 laptop. I think a more realistic title should be 'the $100 gadget.' The problem is that gadgets have not been successful."[4] Others thought Negroponte was naively ambitious. He simply forged ahead.

To achieve his dream, Negroponte needed a strategy to do three things: (1) design the computer, (2) have it manufactured inexpensively, and (3) get it into the hands of children around the world by selling it (at cost) to developing nations.[5] The first was the easiest. Though the people on his team faced their share of setbacks and delays, they made progress fairly quickly. They overcame the second hurdle when they found a manufacturer.

At that point, Negroponte thought everything else would fall quickly in place. But he grossly underestimated the difficulty of the third task. He planned to work directly with the ministries of education of seven key countries: China, India, Thailand, Egypt, Nigeria, Brazil, and Argentina. Without employing a sales and marketing team, he would convince them to buy seven to ten million machines the first year. Once the first wave of computers was in place, he reasoned, the rest of the world would follow, and the next year they would sell one hundred to two hundred million computers.

It didn't happen that way. Orders did not pour in. They needed help. OLPC needed to transition from dreamers to strategic implementers. To do that, they enlisted the aid of Brightstar, a Miami-based mobile device manufacturer and distributor that was already working with them on another initiative. They have experience in areas that Negroponte and his colleagues don't. Negroponte admits:

> Most of the people in these offices [at OLPC's headquarters] are not qualified by their experience to make that transition. We're good at new ideas and being disruptive and so on and so forth. So that's one of the reasons we shifted basically all of what we would be calling sales and marketing to Miami. They are people who have lots of experience doing that sort of thing and the whole logistic side, basically from the end of the factory to the schoolroom door. . . . Those [strategic processes] are run by people who

actually wear suits, and know that world, whether it's the political world or the business world.[6]

Negroponte has not given up on his dream. He has revised his strategy. He's willing to do what it takes. As author and technology journalist Robert Buderi observes, Negroponte has "the skills, contacts, energy, and chutzpah to go for it. He's a wealthy man, from a powerful family. He's 63 now. He's already achieved fame as the founder of the MIT Media Lab. But instead of sitting back, relaxing, and enjoying life, he decided to stand up and enjoy life in a different way—by working his butt off for a world-changing dream."[7]

As I write this, he hasn't accomplished it yet. But he's still working at it. In 2007, mass production of the computers began in November. In December, Peru ordered 260,000 units.[8] Another 190,000 units were purchased through a program in the United States where buyers could get one XO for themselves and have another donated to a child in a developing country. In the coming years, we'll have to watch to see whether Negroponte and OLPC can develop and implement a strategy that's as big as their dream.

WHAT'S YOUR PLAN?

Do you have a strategy to reach your dream? How do you answer the Pathway Question? Are you trying to work it out? Or are you waiting for someone like a fairy godmother to bail you out? If you're like some animated characters in Disney movies who wish upon a star and simply wait and hope it will come true, you're going to be disappointed!

It's sad when people don't have dreams. It's equally sad when they have dreams but no strategy to reach them, no way to make the climb up to them or build the foundation under them. Over the years I have tried to be a dream lifter. I'm an encourager by nature. I love motivating people to dream because I believe too many people shoot too low in life. But sometimes when I talk to people and ask them to share their dreams with me, I see that they're missing a connection between where they are and where they want to go.

"That is a great dream!" I say in response to the picture they paint. Then I ask, "How are you going to accomplish it?" Some have no idea. That can be okay if, like in Mike Hyatt's case (in chapter 2), their dream is brand-new and they have only just begun to work on strategy. But if I see them six months or a year or five years later and they still have no strategy, then they're in trouble. They've failed to make the transition from dreamer to implementer.

There is no magic power in having a dream. You can't just wait for it. You have to work for it. And you need to have a strategy that gives direction and focus to that work. The reason I wrote this book was to give you a realistic shot at reaching your dream. Remember, the more yeses you can answer to the ten questions about your dream, the better the odds that you will achieve your dream. The Pathway Question is the hinge pin for the entire idea. If you have a strategy for reaching your dream, you have an excellent shot at achieving it. If not, you might as well be living in Fantasyland.

> *There is no magic power in having a dream.*
> *You can't just wait for it. You have to work for it.*

A friend recently acquainted me with the results of a 2005 study published by ThinkTQ, a training and publishing organization. It illustrates how infrequently people develop strategies for achieving their dreams. Here is what the study revealed about the people tested:

- 26 percent focus on specific, tangible targets for what they want in life.
- 19 percent set goals aligned with their purpose, mission, and passion.
- 15 percent write down all their goals in specific measurable detail.
- 12 percent maintain a clearly defined goal for every major interest and life role.
- 12 percent identify related daily, weekly, and long-term goals with deadlines.
- 7 percent take daily action toward the attainment of at least one goal.[9]

The study's authors comment that "Americans, once again, get an 'F' in this critical area of their performance. Simply put, they fail to consistently take the . . . actions necessary to move their dreams and visions out of their hearts and heads and into their lives." The bottom line is that most people fail to take action to achieve their dreams. And that failure is the result of very little strategic planning.

HOW TO SECURE YOUR DREAM

English novelist Mary Webb advised, "Saddle your dreams before you ride them." What does that mean? It means we need to plan to plan. A strategy is as important a part of the dream as the dream itself. Most people would agree that planning is important. However, they still neglect to do it. They forget to make it part of the process. We're so busy stargazing that we neglect strategizing.

My goal in this chapter is to help you plan to plan. Because every dream is unique, I cannot give you specifics. However, I can give you an approach to planning that can assist you. This is my approach, based on the word *secure.* I hope you find it helpful and memorable:

STATE ALL YOUR POSITIONS

The process of reaching your dream is like reaching a destination using a GPS (Global Positioning System) device. If it knows where you are and you tell it where you want to go, it can create a map for you. The difference between a GPS and you is that you have to create all of your turn-by-turn directions yourself. American novelist Mark Twain insisted, "The secret of getting ahead is getting started. The secret of getting started is breaking your complex, overwhelming tasks into small, manageable tasks, and then starting on the first one."

> *"The secret of getting ahead is getting started. The secret of getting started is breaking your complex, overwhelming tasks into small manageable tasks, and then starting on the first one."*
> —MARK TWAIN

When I want to create a plan to achieve a dream, I start by stating my positions in the process . . .

1. My present position. First, I ask myself, Where am I right now? I have to be honest about my present situation. It is impossible for me to ignore the reality of my present position and be successful. If I am not certain of my current position related to my dream, then I will ask people who can help me figure it out.

Former General Electric CEO Jack Welch observed, "Strategy is first trying to understand where you sit in today's world. Not where you wish you were or where you hoped you would be, but where you are. Then it's trying to understand where you want to be five years out. Finally, it's assessing the realistic chances of getting from there to there."

If you're like most people, you may not be thrilled with your starting point. But as you consider your present position, take heart from the words of Richard Evans, who wrote *The Christmas Box.* He said, "Everyone who got to where they are had to begin where they were."

2. My future position. Next, I put into words where I want to go. I do this by asking, *What will my dream look like when I have achieved it?* Identifying my future position gives me direction and motivation to go after my dream. Millionaire industrialist Henry J. Kaiser, the founder of Kaiser Aluminum as well as the Kaiser-Permanente healthcare system, asserted, "The evidence is overwhelming that you cannot begin to achieve your best unless you set some aim in life."

> "The evidence is overwhelming that you cannot begin
> to achieve your best unless you set some aim in life."
> —HENRY J. KAISER

3. The positions in between. Then I try to figure out the pathway that lies between by asking, *What steps must I take to get from my present position to my future one?* You must set a series of small goals to get where you want to go. As friend and author Dick Biggs points out, "Your dream is a general idealistic view of where you would like to go. But your goals are specific, realistic declarations of how you are going to get there."

As you begin to write out the steps you expect to take to reach your dream, don't expect to be able to follow them quickly and easily. Plans are clear and simple. Life and the pursuit of dreams are messy. Creating the process is a start, and it gets you going, but it is far from being an exact science. Filmmaker George Lucas commented, "Setting realistic goals is one of the hardest things to do, because you don't always know exactly where you're going, and you shouldn't. For me, just setting the goals of getting decent grades in school and taking subjects I had some interest in was a big goal, and I focused on that."[10]

Many people mistakenly believe that they're finished with the Pathway Question as soon as they know where they are, know where they want to go, and have identified steps that can take them there. But if that were true, more people would be achieving their dreams. There's more to strategy than just steps. And that leads us to the next thing you must do in the process after stating your positions.

Examine All Your Actions

The real difference between a dream and wishful thinking is what you do day to day. John Ruskin, an English author, art critic, and social commentator, said, "What we think, or what we know, or what we believe is, in the end, of little consequence. The only consequence is what we do." To reach your dream, you must . . .

1. *Do something.* The process starts by doing something—doing *anything* if you are a naturally sedentary person or someone who is discouraged. Declaration of Independence signer John Hancock asserted, "All worthwhile people have good thoughts, good ideas, and good intentions, but precious few of them ever translate those into action."

> *The real difference between a dream and wishful thinking is what you do day to day.*

In the beginning, you just need to get moving. Try different things. It's much easier to start doing something *right* if you've already started doing *something.* Dennis Bakke, cofounder and former CEO of U.S. electric power distribution firm AES, once said, "We try a bunch of stuff, we see what works, and we call that our strategy." In other words, if you don't know *exactly* what to do, don't let it keep you from doing *something.*

2. *Do something* today *that relates to your dream.* Runner, author, and cardiologist George Sheehan observed, "There are those of us who are always about to live. We are waiting until things change, until there is more time, until we are less tired, until we get a promotion, until we settle down—until, until, until. It always seems as if there is some major event that must occur in our lives before we

begin living." If you want to achieve your dreams, you cannot allow yourself to be one of those people! How do you avoid it? By doing something that will advance you toward your dream *today*.

TV news journalist and *Hardball* host Chris Matthews advises, "Whatever your ambitions, whatever the field you want to enter, if you want to play a game, go to where it's played. If you want to be a lawyer, go to law school. If you can't get into the best law school, get into the best one you can. Same with medical or business school or whatever. If you want to get into TV, get yourself a job, any job in the business. The important thing is to get your seat at the table."[11] He knows because when he wanted to work in the world of politics, he went to Washington, D.C., and knocked on doors of congressional offices to land a job—any job—to get started. Eventually a senator found him a position answering difficult letters for a few hours a day and then working the three-to-eleven shift as a Capitol police officer. It wasn't where he wanted to end up, but it was a start.

If you're really serious about wanting to achieve your dream, what can you do *today* that will take you a step closer to achieving it? You can't reach your dream all at once. You have to get there in steps, and the only time you can actually take a step is *today*. Follow the advice of German philosopher Johann Wolfgang von Goethe, who said,

> Each indecision brings its own delays
> And days are lost lamenting over lost days.
> What you can do or think you can do, begin it.
> For boldness has magic, power and genius in it.

3. Do something every day that relates to your dream. Personal growth proponent Earl Nightingale remarked, "We read about people who sail around the world in a thirty-foot sailboat or overcome handicaps to win a gold medal at the Olympics, and we later find they're stories about persistence." I would take that one step further and suggest that they are stories of *focused* persistence. The secret to your success is found in your daily agenda. If you do the right things day after day, then you will make progress, and you will eventually achieve what you set out to do. And that's what matters.

CONSIDER ALL YOUR OPTIONS

World War II general George S. Patton Jr. declared "Successful generals make plans to fit circumstances, but do not try to create circumstances to fit plans." Once you figure out a plan for reaching your dream—the intermediate steps you think will get you there—there is a danger that you will become inflexible and try to stick to your plan no matter what. Sometimes it's wiser to explore other options. When you are having a hard time moving forward, don't be quick to revise your dream. Instead, revise your plan.

> *"Successful generals make plans to fit circumstances,*
> *but do not try to create circumstances to fit plans."*
> —GEORGE S. PATTON JR.

Peter Drucker, who is often called the father of modern management, understood the uncertainty of strategic planning. It's not an exact science. And anyone who engages in the process of creating a pathway to reach his dream must understand the importance of remaining flexible in the process. Drucker stated, "Strategic planning is necessary precisely because we cannot forecast. . . . Strategic planning does not deal with future decisions. It deals with the futurity of present decisions. Decisions exist only in the present. The question that faces the strategic decision-maker is not what his organization should do tomorrow. It is: 'What do we have to do today to be ready for an uncertain tomorrow?'"[12] The best way to face the uncertainty of tomorrow is to consider our options as events unfold.

I have observed that the situation often determines the best strategy. Just as many quarterbacks in football are empowered by their coaches to call an audible and select a different play when they size up the defense at the line of scrimmage, we need to be ready to make changes in order to achieve our goals. A rigid mind-set doesn't serve well when we're trying to achieve our dreams.

Sam Walton, the founder of Wal-Mart, has often been credited with being a visionary leader. His dream was to provide value to customers so that it would improve their lives. But he was notorious for changing his plans and abandoning strategies that didn't work. Sam's son Jim Walton admitted, "We all snickered at some writers who viewed Dad as a grand strategist who intuitively developed complex plans and implemented them with precision. Dad thrived on change, and no decision was ever sacred."[13]

> "However beautiful the strategy, you should occasionally look at the results."
> —WINSTON CHURCHILL

I love what British prime minister Winston Churchill, a gifted orator and an inspired leader, said about strategy: "However beautiful the strategy, you should occasionally look at the results." The results matter. What good is a masterfully planned strategy that doesn't yield positive results?

UTILIZE ALL YOUR RESOURCES

I think every writer dreams of having a best-selling book. I know that was true for me. By 1997, I'd written a dozen books, and though I had helped quite a few people, I wasn't making the impact I desired. I believe that many authors write a book, send it to a publisher, and then hope. The only problem: hope is not a strategy. I knew that if I was to have any chance at making it to a bestseller list, I needed a plan.

As a leader, I naturally think in terms of resources. I know that the more resources that come into play to achieve any goal, the greater the chances of success. So I took stock, and here's my evaluation of what I had:

- ⊛ *A really good idea for a book.* It may sound obvious, but it all starts here. You have to create something of value to be a successful author. You can't go into the process asking, "How can I sell enough books to be a bestseller?" You have to ask, "What can I write that will help people so much that it could become a bestseller?" My answer was *The 21 Irrefutable Laws of Leadership.* I believed this book could add value to people who wanted to learn about leadership.
- ⊛ *An excellent team.* By this time, I was surrounded by excellent

people. I had a good writer. I had a wonderful publisher, Thomas Nelson, which wanted to see me succeed. And I had my own company, which was highly experienced at putting on events. NBA coach Pat Riley offers this view about teamwork: "Teamwork requires that everyone's efforts flow in a single direction. Feelings of significance happen when a team's energy takes on a life of its own." All the people on these teams were ready and willing to work together to accomplish the goal of trying to get this book on the bestseller list.

⊛ *A deadline.* To do great and important tasks, two things are necessary: a plan and not quite enough time. A deadline pushes you to accomplish something by a designated end point. We knew that if we would have any chance of being noticed by the publishing industry, we needed to get people to buy books during a small window of time.

⊛ *Creativity.* As our two teams brainstormed how to sell a lot of books in a short period, great ideas surfaced. We finally decided to do a fifteen-city book tour in five days. We chartered a jet, took care of the logistics to host free events in the cities, invited local bookstores to sell books at the events, and did a bunch of publicity. And when everything was arranged, off we went to Tampa, Atlanta, Charlotte, Washington, D.C., Pittsburgh, Columbus, Indianapolis, Grand Rapids, St. Louis, Dallas, Oklahoma City, Denver, San Jose, Los Angeles, and San Diego.

⊛ *Opportunity.* All of that was a lot of work, but it only gave us the opportunity to get in front of people. They still had to make the choice to buy the book. In each city, I planned to teach from *The 21 Irrefutable Laws of Leadership*, and individuals would have a chance to buy the book from representatives of a local bookstore. Fortunately, people loved it. Many business owners in attendance bought books by the case to train their leaders. And they talked to others about the books and got sales going. At the end of the month, *The 21 Irrefutable Laws of Leadership* made it onto three bestseller lists. It remained on one business book list for twenty-three months! Eleven years later, that book has sold more than 2 million copies.

Think about your dream. You may not want to write books. Maybe you want to win an Olympic medal or build a great company or raise your children so that they reach their potential. No matter the dream, it will require resources. What's available to you? What assets do you possess? Who can help you? Stop and make a list. It's not enough just to plan. You need to engage every resource you have in order to make your dream come true.

REMOVE ALL YOUR NONESSENTIALS

Think about your dream for a moment. Think about everything that will result from it. If you're like most people, what come to mind are the benefits you will receive, the places you will go, the people you will meet, the things you will own, and the position or title you will earn. Do you notice anything peculiar about that list? It contains only the value that will be *added* to you. It contains none of the things you will have to *give up* to achieve it. However, if you want to go up, there will be things you must give up.

Big dreams come with a price. When you reach chapter 7, "The Cost Question," you'll learn more about that. But remember this:

you *will* have to give up things to achieve your dream. And the greatest challenge isn't giving up the obvious things that will hurt you. It will be giving up the good things that you like but won't help you. For example, a friend loves golf but hasn't played it in more than fifteen years because his children are young and it takes too much time away from them. I delegate many tasks I enjoy doing because someone else can do them nearly as well as I do. I enjoy doing research, but I've given much of it to my staff. There are things that *only* I can do. On them I focus.

Removing nonessentials from your daily routine will be a constant struggle, but it is worth fighting for. Why? Because most people who fail to reach their dream aren't stopped because an insurmountable barrier confronted them. No, they often become worn out trying to carry too many things on their journey. If you want to reach your dream, you need to let go of the things that don't really matter so that you can accomplish the things that really do.

Embrace All Your Challenges

Once you've stated all your positions, examined all your actions, considered all your options, utilized all your resources, and removed all your nonessentials, you still have one more thing to do: embrace all your challenges. King Solomon, considered to be the wisest man who ever lived, wrote, "A sensible man watches for problems ahead and prepares to meet them. The simpleton never looks, and suffers the consequences."[14]

The pathway to every dream is filled with challenges. Expect them. Better yet, prepare yourself to face them. Wouldn't you rather look ahead and prepare than have to look back and regret? You can probably envision your dream. Now envision yourself overcoming some of the challenges you will face. The first is failure. Everyone experiences failure in pursuit of dreams. One of your goals is to keep hanging on to your dream through your failures until you finally become successful.

I met sports psychologist Rob Gilbert several years ago when I was doing leadership training with the coaches at the University of North Carolina and Duke. Over dinner, I asked Rob what separated athletes who were successful from those who were not. His answer was simple and profound: "Those who lose visualize the penalties of failure. Those who win visualize the rewards of success."

> *"Those who lose visualize the penalties of failure.*
> *Those who win visualize the rewards of success."*
> —ROB GILBERT

Since you will experience failure, I suggest that you make it your friend. I believe that so strongly that I wrote a book on the subject called *Failing Forward*. When failure happens, you need to embrace it. Examine it. Learn from it. If you do, you won't keep repeating the same mistake again, and you will also become emotionally strong as a result.

The second challenge you will need to face and overcome is inflexibility. Retired army general Wesley K. Clark noted, "There are only two kinds of plans. Plans that might work and plans that won't work. There's no such thing as the perfect plan. You have to take a plan that might work and make it work."[15]

> *"There are only two kinds of plans. Plans that might work and plans that won't work. . . . You have to take a plan that might work and make it work."*
> —WESLEY K. CLARK

As you work to remain flexible, remember that while the dream may stay the same, everything else is subject to change: timelines, resources, assumptions, plans, and team members. Comedian Bill Cosby's quip, "Nothing fits a pigeonhole but a pigeon," is humorous but true. Remain flexible and be ready to change. And be ready to employ two skill sets: critical thinking that asks, *What needs to be changed?* and creative thinking that asks, *How can we change it?* If you can remain flexible and use such thinking, you have a good chance of facing challenges and overcoming obstacles.

There is no guarantee that you will be able to SECURE your dream by following these steps. However, if you have a plan, remain flexible, focus your efforts, gather your resources, and work hard every day to move closer to your dream, you have a good chance of reaching your dream. As you put your strategy into practice and walk the pathway toward your dream, remember the Italian proverb: "Between saying and doing many a pair of shoes is worn out."

Dreams don't come quickly or easily. And the rewards often don't come until very late. So hang in there and keep working. To achieve your dream, you need to start well, and you need to finish well.

CAN YOU ANSWER YES TO THE PATHWAY QUESTION: DO I HAVE A STRATEGY TO REACH MY DREAM?

As you consider your strategy for reaching your dream, use the acronym—SECURE—to help you with the planning process:

State all your positions:

What is your starting point?

What is your ending point?

What steps do you expect to lie between?

Examine all your actions:

What actions must you take every day to get closer to your dream?

Consider all your options:

What parts of your strategy are you willing to alter to move forward?

Utilize all your resources:

What resources do you have at your disposal? (List everything you can think of.)

Remove all your nonessentials:

What activities are you currently engaged in that do not contribute to the journey toward your dream?

Embrace all your challenges:

What problems, obstacles, and failures do you expect to face in your dream journey?

What can you do to avoid what may be avoidable?

What can you do to prepare yourself to meet your challenges?

What must you do to prepare yourself for failure?

Use your answers to the above questions to write out (1) daily disciplines, (2) monthly goals, and (3) a long-term (multiyear) plan. Then follow it. But remember, you *will* have to change it in the coming weeks, months, and years. That's okay. Every time you change it, you're improving it and increasing your chances for success.

CHAPTER 6

The People Question
*Have I Included the People
I Need to Realize My Dream?*

*It marks a big step in your development when
you come to realize that other people can help
you do a better job than you can do alone.*

—ANDREW CARNEGIE

No matter what your dream is—whether as artist or entrepreneur, politician or Nobel Prize winner—you will be interacting with other people. Unless your dream is to work in a vacuum and be unknown to everyone, you'll have to learn to work with others as partners or patrons, bosses or colleagues, clients or constituents, customers or critics. People may be a big factor or a small one, depending on what you desire to do. But no matter what, you will have to include people if you want to realize your dream.

It didn't take me long to learn this truth. I accepted my first leadership position in 1969 mere weeks after graduating from college and getting married to my wife, Margaret. I had big dreams of building a large, influential church. However, that first job was at a small church in rural Indiana that didn't have many financial resources. When Margaret and I met with the church's leaders, they offered me a salary of eighty dollars a week and told me that I was free to pursue additional work to make ends meet.

"No," Margaret said to the leaders. "Even if the salary is part-time, John will give all his energy to the church full-time. He is going to become a great leader."

Margaret took on three jobs to keep us afloat financially; she taught kindergarten, worked part-time in a jewelry store, and cleaned houses. I'm grateful to Margaret for so many things, and she has been vital to my dream journey. But I will never forget the empowerment I felt when she stood up for me and my dream that day so early in our marriage. None of my dreams would have come true without her.

HELP ALONG THE WAY

According to pastor and friend Chris Hodges, "A dream is a compelling vision you see in your heart that's too big to accomplish without the help of others." I have found that to be true in my life. I could not have fulfilled any of my dreams without the help of others. The list of people who have made a difference in my life is long. Literally hundreds and hundreds of people have helped me to live out my dreams. Some have inspired me. Others have come alongside me to help. Many have adopted my dreams as their own. All have made a difference and added value to my life in ways that I cannot adequately express. Each person is very special to me, and I am so grateful for all of the help.

> *"A dream is a compelling vision you see in your heart
> that's too big to accomplish without the help of others."*
> —CHRIS HODGES

If you want to realize your dream, you need a team to help you. It's hard to list all the things a team can do for you. There are so many. Recently I tried to put into words how my team helps me. Here's what I wrote:

My team makes me better than I am.

My team multiplies my value to others.

My team enables me to do what I do best.

My team allows me to help others do their best.

My team gives me more time.

My team provides me with companionship.

My team helps me fulfill the desires of my heart.

My team compounds my vision and effort.

My team empowers me to realize my dream.

Without my team, I would not be able to do anything of significance.

WHO SHOULD BE ON YOUR DREAM TEAM?

How do you answer the People Question, which asks, Have I included the people I need to realize my dream? When I talk to people who have passion and a clear picture of their dream, I always ask them who they have enlisted to help them achieve it. Most good leaders know that they cannot accomplish their dreams on their own, and they start naming the people who are working with them. But some people seem dumbfounded by the question. It never occurs to them that they will need the assistance of others to achieve their dreams.

Here is what I have found to be true:

Some people have a dream but no team—their dream is impossible.

Some people have a dream but a bad team—their dream is a nightmare.

Some people have a dream and are building a team—their dream has potential.

Some people have a dream and a great team—their dream is inevitable.

It's not enough to have a dream. You must also have a dream team.

> *It's not enough to have a dream.*
> *You must also have a dream team.*

People recognize this truth in sports. They understand that they cannot win without the right players. But it also applies to every other aspect of life. If you want to achieve your dream, you need others willing to come alongside you and work with you. That was true for Arnold Schwarzenegger, whom I wrote about in the chapter on the Ownership Question. He gives a great deal of credit to Reg

Park, who inspired him; Franco Columbu, his close friend and workout partner since the early days in Munich; Joe Weider, who helped him go to the next level of bodybuilding in the United States; Charlotte Parker, his publicist, who promoted him tirelessly; and, of course, Maria Shriver, his wife, for her unconditional support.

That's been true of Mike Hyatt, whom I wrote about in the chapter on the Clarity Question. Without his team, he never would have turned his division around and made it the most productive in the company, nor would he have become Thomas Nelson's CEO.

Andy Hull, the young musician in the chapter dealing with the Reality Question, relies on his band mates every day as they perform together. And he told me how crucial it was for him to partner with the right record label, the right attorney, and the right manager. The community he is creating is *the reason* he does what he does.

Bob Taylor wouldn't be successful without his longtime partner Kurt Listug or the key people on his leadership team or the hundreds of workers who make the guitars.

And Nicholas Negroponte, a technical wizard, has an entire team of brilliant people who developed his laptop for children and another team working to distribute it.

You can examine the story of *any* successful person who has achieved a dream, and you will find that he or she is surrounded by people who helped to make it happen.

Before you answer the People Question, you may be asking a question of your own: What kind of people should be on your team? That depends on your dream. Several years ago, my friend Walt Kallestad, who is the CEO of the Joy Company, gave me an acrostic identifying the qualities of individuals who should be on someone's dream team. He says that dream team members . . .

Dare to focus on your significance, not simply on your success.

Respond to your ideas with respect, not disgust or contempt.

Expect the best.

Affirm your talents and abilities.

Maximize learning and growth opportunities to improve the dream and the dreamer.

Take time to give honest feedback.

Encourage you unconditionally and nonjudgmentally to help you persevere.

Accept only excellence, since mediocrity kills dreams.

Make the most of your mistakes and failures.

I share Walt's acrostic with you because I think it's a good one. You may want to use it as you seek to answer the People Question. Or you may want to use the three criteria I've developed for dream team members. As you read about them, think about how these kinds of people could help you as you pursue your dream:

My Dream Team Includes People Who Inspire Me

Inspiration often gives birth to dreams, but it is also needed to keep dreams alive! We all need people to encourage us, cheer us on, and lift us to a higher level. Some people simply have that effect on us. When we are with them, they motivate us to live stronger, think better, work harder, and risk more. They compel us to continue!

Robert Schuller has been a dream encourager to millions of people, including me. When my book *Failing Forward* was released, I gave my first copy to him. Over dinner I thanked him for the encouragement he had given me through his books and his kind words. He has often inspired me to overcome disappointments and failures.

One of the things about pursuing dreams is that we often get sidetracked and find ourselves taking unwanted detours. At such times, we need people who will hang in there with us. Many people are very close to my heart because they believed in me when I didn't believe in myself. They listened to me without condemnation and loved me unconditionally, even when I wasn't very lovable. Without them, I wouldn't have possessed the hope I needed to keep pursuing my dream.

My Dream Team Includes People Who Are Honest with Me

I also need people on my dream team who are willing to tell me the truth. That may at first seem contradictory to my desire to include people who inspire me, but that's not the case. I don't look for people who want to knock me down. Rather, I look for people who are willing and able to give me constructive feedback. That's especially important in the area of dreams because, as Greek orator Demosthenes asserted, "Nothing is so easy as to deceive one's self; for what we wish, we readily believe."

Many people never ask for honest feedback from others. I think they fear reality and worry that someone telling them the truth will discourage them so much that they'll give up their dream. But a dream without honest feedback is often little more than make-believe. And a dream that cannot survive honest criticism is a dream that's likely never to be attained.

Early in my career, I was guilty of not asking for the honest opinions of others. Like many people in their twenties, I thought I knew better. But the result was that I did not realize many of my early dreams. However, as I started to become a better leader and my hunger to achieve my dreams intensified, my self-confidence increased. I asked other people questions. And the results were dramatic. I began to grow and improve.

When you're unaware of your shortcomings, you can't fix them! For example, in my first attempts at public speaking, I wasn't very good. I prepared well and tried hard, but my speeches were usually not effective. After a period of frustration, I humbled myself and asked excellent communicators for advice. They often told me things I didn't want to hear. But I needed to listen and learn. And I learned to pay attention to the things that struck a sensitive chord within me; it was often a signal that I was hearing about something I needed to improve. The things that upset me most or that I resisted most were usually what I needed to work on most. And if I gave myself time to reflect on what I was told and seek improvement, I usually improved dramatically.

> *"It takes humility to seek feedback. It takes wisdom to understand it, analyze it and appropriately act on it."*
> —STEPHEN R. COVEY

Author Stephen R. Covey observed, "It takes humility to seek feedback. It takes wisdom to understand it, analyze it and appropriately act on it."[1] It also takes humility to show appreciation for a person's courage to provide honest feedback. And the good news is that if you ask for advice and show appreciation, you send a message that your desire to grow is bigger than your ego and you invite future feedback that will help you continue to improve.

If you want to benefit from the value of having other people on board with your dream, ask for their opinions. Asking and then listening will make an immediate difference.

MY DREAM TEAM INCLUDES PEOPLE WHOSE SKILLS COMPLEMENT MINE

You can't do everything, and neither can I. Successful people seek help from individuals who are skilled in areas other than their own. Most of the people on my dream team are very different from me in their giftedness. Our team may have the same values, vision, and priorities, but each member is different in the area of skills and temperament. As a result, together we accomplish more than we ever would independent of one another. We complement and complete one another.

The kinds of people you need on your team depend on your particular abilities, experience, and temperament. Think about your strategy for achieving your dream. What must be done to achieve it? Which of those things best suit your abilities? Which will require the help of others with different skills? Where will you need people with experience? What kinds of tasks will require a temperament different from yours?

There really is no such thing as a self-made person. People who are successful have had help along the way from others—whether or not they want to acknowledge it. Knowing this truth can free you to admit you need help and begin looking for it. And that's a crucial step in the process of achieving success. The next step is to actually bring those people on board so that they are willing to take the journey toward the dream with you.

TO RECRUIT THE TEAM, TRANSFER THE VISION

I've met a lot of people with big dreams who never achieved them because they were unable to get others to see and buy into their vision. They believed that if the dream was worthy, people would simply line up to be a part of it. Recruiting a team doesn't work that way. People who fall into this trap may be visionary, they may be hardworking, and they may have noble intentions, but they won't succeed if they don't learn how to transfer the vision to others. They are condemned to experience the curse that is reportedly used in Romania, which says, "May you have a brilliant idea, which you know is right, and be unable to convince others."

Author and critic John Ruskin understood the power—and challenge—of communicating vision. He asserted, "The greatest thing a human soul ever does in this world is to *see* something, and tell what it *saw* in a plain way. Hundreds of people can talk for one who can think, but thousands can think for one who can see. To see clearly is poetry, prophecy, and religion—all in one."[2]

Obviously the ability to communicate is important in transferring the dream to others. But it takes more than that. It takes credibility and conviction. Vision casting can be done by good communicators. Dream casting can be done only by people who live and breathe their dream. Convincing others of the significance of your dream can happen only if *you* are convinced of the significance of your dream. It requires the right message, spoken by the right messenger, to the right audience. Psychologist, author, and speaker Larry Crabb describes this convergence, saying, "A vision we give to others of who and what they could become has power when it echoes what the spirit has already spoken into their souls." That power can convince people to join you in the pursuit of your dream, and it greatly enhances your chances for success.

So how do you transfer the vision for your dream and do so with power? There is an ancient Chinese saying: "The will is like a cart being pulled by two horses: the mind and the emotions. Both horses need to be moving in the same direction to pull the cart forward." I agree with that, and I believe a third "horse" comes into play: visualization. To communicate with people and connect them effectively with your dream, you need to do it logically, emotionally, and visually.

> *To communicate with people and connect them effectively with your dream, you need to do it logically, emotionally, and visually.*

1. TRANSFER THE DREAM LOGICALLY

What people don't believe, they don't buy into. The ability to communicate your dream logically is the first step in gaining credibility with people. If you don't pass this first gate of people's intellect, you will not be able to proceed any further. How do you do that? First, by communicating a realistic understanding of the situation today. Every time you communicate vision to people, the first thing the skeptics ask is, "But what about . . . ?" If they don't ask it out loud, they say it to themselves. And they will keep asking it until you have addressed all their concerns.

You need to demonstrate that you understand the situation at least as well as they do. That requires being extremely thorough when sharing your dream and not dwelling on its positive benefits to the exclusion of the facts. Remember, when Mike Hyatt communicated his dream of turning around his division at Thomas Nelson, he laid all his cards on the table. He let everyone know that *he* knew how bad everything was.

The second thing you need to do when transferring the vision logically is to provide a sound strategy. Good strategy always breaks the dream down to manageable parts. If a dream seems too large and unattainable, people become discouraged and lose interest quickly. When big dreams are broken into smaller pieces and different pieces are given to individual champions, the tasks seem more attainable, and each person involved has an increased sense of personal ownership and involvement.

There is a real art to communicating all of this information effectively without getting bogged down in details or boring people. You have to give enough information to satisfy most people but not so much that you lose them. It takes skills and it takes practice. But to transfer the vision, you must learn to do it.

2. Transfer the Dream Emotionally

When you can present your dream logically, people will often stop resisting it. But that doesn't mean they will step forward to embrace it. To get them to connect with your dream, you need to connect with them emotionally. What people don't feel, they don't buy into.

Here's how you can connect people to your dream on an emotional level:

Show them the dream from their perspective. It's said that the great philosopher-poet Ralph Waldo Emerson and his son struggled and strained when trying to wrestle a young calf into their barn. Drenched with sweat and at the end of their rope, they were ready to give up when an Irish servant girl came by. She walked over to the calf, stuck her finger into the animal's mouth, and the calf, associating the sensation with her mother, peacefully followed the girl into the barn.

People are not that different from that calf. You can push them, you can prod them, and they may never do what you want. But help them to feel that they will benefit, and they are likely to go along. People do things for their own reasons—not my reasons or yours. And their reasons are almost always tied to their emotions.

I love the story of Michael Faraday, inventor of the first electric motor, presenting his new device to British prime minister William Gladstone. Hoping to gain support of the government, Faraday showed a crude model—a wire wrapped around a magnet. Gladstone showed little interest.

"What good is it?" the statesman asked Faraday.

"Someday you will be able to tax it," replied the scientist. Faraday could have explained the physics of his invention. He could have explained its practical applications. But instead he appealed to the politician's interests.

I don't know whether that story is true, but it teaches a truth just the same. If you want to win people over to your dreams, you need to speak in the language of their interests, not your own.

Show them your heart. Just because people want to know what's in it for them when you share your dream, that doesn't mean they lack interest in what it means to you. People buy into the dreamer before they buy into the dream. To transfer the dream emotionally, you need to let people see your heart and your hope. Sharing your heart tells your story. Sharing your hope tells the story of your dream and how it will impact the future.

> *People buy into the dreamer before they buy into the dream.*

You may be able to communicate the idea of your dream in a matter of minutes. But it will take you a lot longer to convince people of where your heart is. It will require patience on your part. And waiting until people engage at the heart level isn't a sign of weakness. It's a sign of wisdom. Strength lies not in streaking ahead but in adapting one's stride to the slower pace of others while continuing to lead. If we run too far ahead, we lose our power to influence.

Marketing and sales experts say that people generally need to hear an idea seven times before they will embrace it and call it their own idea. And the time necessary for this ownership varies, depending on the person. Roughly speaking . . .

10 percent of people are pioneers,

70 percent are settlers, and

20 percent are antagonists.

Make it your goal to win over the pioneers and wait for the settlers. If you communicate your heart well, live it with integrity, and wait for the timing to be right, your dream will gain credibility and go from a good idea to a great one in their eyes. And when you're ready to move forward, do so with the 80 percent and try your best to leave the antagonists behind.

Show them the benefits. Author and social commentator Studs Terkel observed, "I think most of us are looking for a calling, not a job. Most of us, like the assembly line worker, have jobs that are too small for our spirit. Jobs are not big enough for people."[3] Dreams, however, are big enough.

A grand dream benefits everyone. Your job is to help people see the benefits. You need to help them connect with the opportunities for achieving personal growth, finding fulfillment, and increasing their self-esteem. You need to provide them with every reason you have for joining you. And if you can't offer plenty of legitimate reasons about why they should be involved, then you have no business trying to recruit them to your team in the first place.

3. TRANSFER THE DREAM VISUALLY

After you help people to understand the dream logically and to connect with it emotionally, the final step in transferring the dream is to make it real to them visually. You need to really bring it to life. Why? Because what people don't see, they don't buy into.

Novelist Leo Tolstoy said, "We should show life neither as it is or ought to be, but only as we see it in our dreams." We can do that by painting verbal pictures. We can do it by using photographs or film. We can use music. But the most compelling picture is our living what we are trying to communicate.

> *"We should show life neither as it is or*
> *ought to be, but only as we see it in our dreams."*
> —LEO TOLSTOY

In all honesty, people can be reluctant to embrace a big dream. Even the people who say they desire a dream often don't really want the dream. They want the *results* of the dream. Look at all the commercials for diets and diet products. People see the before and after pictures, and they want the "after." They're not really interested in the process it takes to get there. If they were, there would be fewer overweight people. However, if we live our dream, practice integrity, and achieve a degree of success, people see what the dream has done for us, and that makes them want it too. If you do everything within your power to live your dream, you become a living advertisement for it. And few things are more compelling to others than that.

If you are successful in transferring the dream, then you'll know it. People will enjoy being part of the team. They will serve one another and you joyfully. They will add value to the team by contributing their creativity. And they will take responsibility for getting things done all by themselves. If you do a good enough job of transferring the vision, the people will eventually take ownership of the dream. But you will have to hold on to the dream loosely for that to happen. What's really powerful is that the team will not only help you to accomplish the dream—team members will add to it and make it bigger and better. When that happens, the dream becomes bigger than you or the team.

I was reminded of what happens when a team adopts a dream by a quote from one of my heroes, John Wooden, the former coach of the UCLA basketball team. He says,

> During my coaching years and ever since, I have made a point of refraining from referring to the UCLA Bruins as "my team" or the individuals on it as "my players." I followed the same policy as varsity coach at Indiana State Teachers College and South Bend Central High School.
>
> When asked, "How did you win that game, Coach?" I would correct the reporter and say, "I didn't win the game. The players did. Our team outscored the opponent."
>
> This may be a small issue, but it is important to me because it reflects my idea that a team is "owned" by its members. The UCLA Bruins was not *my* team. It was *our* team.
>
> I was the head coach—part of a team whose members enjoyed joint ownership.[4]

Coach Wooden transferred his dream of integrity and excellence to every person who played basketball for him. He did it by giving logical reasons for everything the players did, helping them connect to it emotionally, and showing them visually by living it before them every day. And because they bought into his vision and dreams, those players realized many of their own dreams.

DREAM CASTER

For years I have studied great leaders and communicators to learn how they go about sharing their dreams and inviting people to buy in. Nobody did that better than Winston Churchill. An American veteran who was part of the D-Day invasion described meeting Churchill prior to the launch of that bloody offensive against the Nazis. He said that D-Day was the most frightening experience of his life. "In fact," he said, "I don't think some of us would have been able to do what we did, if it weren't for a visit we got just before we crossed the English Channel."

That visit was from Churchill, just hours before they left for the beaches of Normandy. Churchill rode up in a Jeep, got out, and mingled with the troops. "He shook hands with us and even hugged some of us," the veteran recalled. "He spoke of his own wartime experience and identified with our emotions. Then, he stood up in his Jeep and gave a five-minute speech. He spoke the whole time with tears in his eyes." And what did Churchill say on that occasion, knowing that so many young men were going into battle and facing death? He said,

> Gentlemen—I know you are afraid. I remember being afraid when I was a soldier. I had the privilege of defending my country for a number of years through dark days when we didn't know whether we could accomplish what we had been given to do. But this is your moment. We are counting on you to rise to the occasion and achieve everything you have set out to do. The fate of the free world rests on your shoulders. May this be your finest hour.[5]

"Needless to say," the veteran commented, "our group of frightened soldiers turned into a band of men who were ready to take on anybody."

Whenever he spoke, Churchill inspired his listeners. He spoke the truth with dynamic power, connecting with people logically and emotionally. And with the skills of a wordsmith, he painted vivid verbal images. (For example, he coined the phrase *iron curtain*.) If you can learn from communicators such as Churchill and follow their example, people will understand your vision and connect with you. And if you consistently live out what you say, you'll go far in your efforts to win people to your cause and include them in your dream.

IT TAKES A TEAM TO REALIZE A DREAM

So how do you answer the People Question? Have you included the people you need to realize your dream? We cannot achieve our dreams alone. And we owe thanks to the people who choose to join with us to achieve them. We are all dependent on one another. As jazz musician George Adams asserted, "We are made up of thousands of others. Everyone who has ever done a kind deed for us, or spoken one word of encouragement to us, has entered into the makeup of our character and of our thoughts, as well as our success."

> *The size of your dream determines the size of the people who will be attracted to it.*

I don't know what your dream is. I don't know what you desire to accomplish or who you will need to include to see your dream come to fruition. You may need only the encouragement and care of one other human being to help you keep going. Or you may need an army.

Regardless of your situation, I can tell you that you do need others. The bigger the dream, the greater your need. But here's the good news: the size of your dream determines the size of the people who will be attracted to it. If you have a very big dream, you have even greater potential for good people to help you. What you need to do is connect with them, invite them in, transfer the vision, and turn them loose.

CAN YOU ANSWER YES TO THE PEOPLE QUESTION: HAVE I INCLUDED THE PEOPLE I NEED TO REALIZE MY DREAM?

The process of recruiting a team to help you accomplish your dream is never ending. Even those who have already worked hard to do it need to keep working at it. Why? Because a dream is a moving target. Conditions will be constantly changing, and so will your intermediate goals. As you grow, your personal needs will keep changing too. And the reality is that people come and go; the people who start the journey with you rarely finish it with you.

You need to ask yourself, *Who is currently on my team?* Make a list and include colleagues, mentors, inner circle members, key employees, immediate family, close friends, and so on.

Next, sort them into the three categories I mentioned in the chapter along with a fourth category:

- People who inspire me
- People who tell me the truth
- People whose skills complement mine
- People who don't fit in the other categories

Now, measure their contribution. What impact do they have on you? First of all, is it positive or negative? Put a plus or minus sign next to each person's name. Then give that impact a value, from -10 to +10.

Here's what their scores mean:

+6 to 10	Someone who will help you achieve your dream—keep that person on your dream team
0 to +5	Someone who will probably not contribute to your dream
-10 to -1	Someone who will actually hinder your progress toward your dream—remove that person from your team

As you review your list, you'll probably see that you have too few people in the first category. That's okay. Now is the time to change that. Start recruiting people to become part of your dream team.

CHAPTER 7

The Cost Question
*Am I Willing to Pay
the Price for My Dream?*

*Always remember that striving and struggle
precede success, even in the dictionary.*

—SARAH BAN BREATHNACH

Dreams are personal. And so are the sacrifices that must be made to achieve them. Most people are unwilling to ask themselves the Cost Question: Am I willing to pay the price for my dream? They avoid the question, avoid the cost, and inadvertently avoid their dream.

There isn't a single person in the world who has achieved a dream without paying a price for it. Some pay with their lives or their freedom. Others pay by giving up options or finances or relationships. I have one friend who learned to count the cost with, of all things, a motorcycle.

THE PRICE OF A DREAM

His name is Kevin Myers, and he is the senior pastor of 12Stone™ Church in Lawrenceville, Georgia. Kevin committed himself to becoming a minister at a young age—when he was only sixteen years old. Since he was a kid, he has also been crazy about motorcycles. He bought his first one, a cheap secondhand bike, in his late teens. He had others in his twenties, and though he loved riding them, he had never owned one of the type he'd always dreamed about: a cruiser.

Kevin has dedicated his life to ministry, yet he is a highly entrepreneurial person. From his teenage years, he had a dream to start a church from scratch and build it into an organization that would make an impact on the community and serve thousands of people. In 1987 when he was twenty-six years old, he launched out, moving from Michigan to Georgia to start the church, one that would exist for the sake of people he describes as "spiritually unresolved." He made sacrifices to do it: leaving behind friends and family, giving up a good church staff job, and entering financial uncertainty. He was willing to pay a price for his dream. But the cost ended up being much greater than he had anticipated.

He had expected quick success, hoping to start with 250 people. That would have been a good size church able to sustain itself financially. Instead, the church floundered. It started with fewer than a hundred people and remained that size for six years. It didn't take long for the church to run through every bit of money it had. Then it drained away all the money Kevin and his wife, Marcia, had previously set aside to buy a house. Then it emptied their personal savings account. They lost their medical coverage, and right after that, one of their kids got sick. Medical bills piled up, and they went into debt. Kevin resorted to doing odd jobs and construction work on the side to try to make ends meet. It looked as if his dream was dead.

It got to be more than Kevin could take. He went back to the boss he had in Michigan and asked for his old job. But his former boss encouraged him to hang in there a little longer, to keep working toward his dream. The process nearly broke Kevin.

TURNING THE CORNER

Then in the church's seventh year, things finally started to turn around. His tiny church started to grow. From its inception, the church had met in rented locations. Kevin saw the modest growth as an opportunity for the church to take a risk; they would buy land and build their first building. It wasn't easy, but the people believed in what they were doing and made sacrifices. And as soon as the building opened, the church grew even more.

Around that same time, Kevin had the opportunity to realize his other dream. When his mother died, she left him a few dollars, which he used to buy his first real street bike. It was something he had wanted for twenty years. It represented freedom for him. Kevin calls motorcycling his "legal drug." When the pressures of leadership got to be too much, he would go for a ride. He also took longer trips on the Blue Ridge Parkway every summer. He found it highly exhilarating. His motorcycle had the added bonus of reminding him of his mother every time he fired it up—a memento of her life and love for him.

After the church moved into its new building, it wasn't long before it started to outgrow its space. Kevin began looking for new land where he could build another, larger facility. Constructing the first building had been a big risk. Now there was an even bigger one. The next phase of growth would require $4 million. Kevin knew raising the money was going to be a struggle. He also knew it was going to cost him personally. Kevin says:

> In moments of honest leadership reflection, I knew we would not realize the dream without more sacrifice. For three months, I wrestled with what this season of the dream was going to cost me personally. I had few material resources to give toward the vision. All I really had was the motorcycle. To most people that would not seem like much. But it had meaning to me down to the soul level.
>
> The decision was stressful and internally tumultuous. For years I had already postponed many desires and hopes for my family. And now the next level of the dream was demanding more from me. I remember when I decided to sign over the deed of my dream motorcycle for the sake of the bigger dream. Vivid is the personal loss I felt. But all the greater I remember how defining it was in my soul. I was now more deeply abandoned to the dream than I had ever been. This was an epic chase after the dream, and it would move forward only at the cost of personal desires. It was a leadership breakthrough for me.[1]

Kevin did not share with others the inner turmoil he felt at that time, but he did make public the fact that he was donating his motorcycle. When he did, the people seemed suddenly to understand that dreams cost you something.

The church ultimately raised the money and built the building. Then as the congregation grew, they expanded it. The growth continued, and it was soon time to figure out the next phase of the dream, the next set of sacrifices that would be required.

KEEP DREAMING, KEEP SACRIFICING

In January 2008, Kevin's church opened a new 110,000-square-foot state-of-the art facility on 69 acres with a 2,600-seat auditorium. Currently the weekend attendance is more than 6,000 people. And they are affecting not only their community, but they are also serving people in other parts of the world. Kevin and the members of his congregation have continued paying a price for their dream. Every time they go to another level, they pay more. But the lesson of the motorcycle will always stay with him. Kevin observes:

> That was the season that I discovered the difference between dreams and mere desires. In my teens and twenties I thought they were the same thing. But when you get deeper into a dream, you have to make greater payments. The trades get tougher. And you realize that giving up some of your desires is the price you pay to pursue dreams, a price you must pay to have even a chance of achieving it.
>
> Some people say they have both dreams and desires, but I doubt it. All they really have is desires that serve themselves. More than likely, if they ever had a dream, they dulled it into something small and self-serving. I believe you have to be willing to sacrifice desires for a dream. I wonder if that's true for all real dreams. If so, then it's much more dangerous and adventurous to dream than most people dare to believe. But it is a great chase! And one that leads to few regrets.[2]

There are still challenges ahead for Kevin because he still has dreams. And because of that, there are still prices that he will have to pay. But he has learned the lesson, thanks to a motorcycle he was willing to give up for the sake of his dream.

> *Every journey toward a dream is personal, and as a result, so is the price that must be paid for it.*

WHAT WILL YOU PAY?

What about you? What have you learned about sacrifice? How do you answer the Cost Question: Am I willing to pay the price for my dream? As I said, every journey toward a dream is personal, and as a result, so is the price that must be paid for it. Because I am unable to sit down with you and ask you about your dream in person, I can't advise you about the specific cost of your dream. But I can tell you a few things that are true for everybody who goes after a dream. Here they are:

1. The Dream Is Free, but the Journey Isn't

Recently my friend Collin Sewell and I were engaged in a conversation about dreams. He remarked that in the beginning, all dreams are obstacle-free. That's true, isn't it? When you first think about a dream, it's fun. Isn't it? You see all the possibilities. You imagine all the potential. It's exciting. At that stage, rarely do you think about the cost. But at some point, you have to make a transition from believer of the dream to buyer of the dream. No dream comes true without somebody paying for it.

> *At some point, you have to make a transition*
> *from believer of the dream to buyer of the dream.*
> *No dream comes true without somebody paying for it.*

If you want to achieve a dream, you have to be willing to do more than just imagine the outcome. You have to be willing to pay a price to take the journey forward. That's why dream believers are in abundance. Dream buyers are rare.

2. The Price Must Be Paid Sooner Than You Think

I think most people realize that there will be some cost for achieving their dream. They have a vague notion that *someday* they will have to pay a price. But they don't realize that it will have to be paid sooner than they think. If you've already started pursuing your dream, then you know what I'm talking about. As soon as you started the journey, I bet the price started to become an issue. Why is that? Because dreams confessed create conflict; dreams begun create crisis.

> *Dream believers are in abundance. Dream buyers are rare.*

The moment you declare your dream and try to move toward it, problems begin to surface. Facing the reality is like having cold water hit you in the face. Not expecting anything like that, many people become discouraged. Some table their dreams, putting them on hold. Others abandon their dreams entirely.

Often I have listened to people in midlife express regret because they backed off from their dream in earlier years: a career not pursued, an opportunity left unseized, a relationship allowed to wither and die. Decades later, they come back to it and think more about it. For some, it's too late. They *can't* achieve their dream at any price. For others, the dream is possible, but the price is much higher.

Dreams are like money. The earlier the buy-in and investment, the more the rewards compound over time. For example, in the financial realm, let's say that you invest $1,000 each year for 10 years beginning at age 25 ($10,000 total invested); by age 65, you'd have $112,537. However, if you invested $1,000 a year beginning at age 35 and continued investing *every year for 30 years* ($30,000 total invested), then at age 65, you'd have only $101,073.[3] Similarly if you start paying for your dream early in your life, you increase the chances of getting a good "return" on your investment. And you might avoid the problem pointed out by comedian and political commentator Al Franken, who, after quoting the old maxim, "No man on his deathbed ever said, 'I wish I had spent more time at the office,'" commented, "How does he know that? I'll bet someone on their deathbed said, 'I wish I had spent more time at the office in my twenties and thirties, I would have had a much better life'—gurgle—dead."

If you didn't start paying the price for your dream in the past, you can't change that. But you do have control over whether you start paying today! If you truly want to achieve your dream and not just imagine it, start investing now. Are you discouraged because the return won't be as great if you start late? I hope not. Just think: what will the return be if you *never* invest? It's better to live your dream in part than to miss the opportunity entirely and regret it later on.

3. THE PRICE WILL BE HIGHER THAN YOU EXPECT

All dreams have a price tag on them, and the cost is almost always higher than a person expects to pay. Never once in my conversations with successful people have I heard the words, "Getting to the top was much easier than I anticipated." Everybody I know who has realized a dream has war stories to tell.

> *Never once in my conversations with successful people have I heard the words, "Getting to the top was much easier than I anticipated."*

Years ago while traveling, I learned the taxi principle: find out the cost before you get in. Although that may be possible when hailing a cab, it's impossible when it comes to achieving dreams. You never know the complete cost up front. You find out what it will be only as you take the journey. That was true for Kevin Myers. He knew he would have to pay. But the cost was much higher than he anticipated. He believes it was worth paying, but it was definitely higher than expected.

Actor Paul Hogan, who portrayed the movie character Crocodile Dundee, was once asked how he became successful. I love his answer: "The secret of my success is that I bit off more than I could chew and chewed as fast as I could." Dreams don't come cheap, and they don't come easy. And the bigger the dream, the bigger the price tag. But the secret to paying for your dream is just to keep chewing.

4. THE PRICE MUST BE PAID MORE THAN ONCE

This truth may come as a surprise to you, but you don't get to pay once and then achieve your dream. You have to pay again and again. I know I was surprised to find that out. When I was younger, I thought it would be like paying an admission fee to an amusement park—pay the price once and then just enjoy the rides. Unfortunately, that's not the way dreams work.

The statement I use to describe the process is this: "You've got to give up to go up." Every time I face another sacrifice, every time I recognize that there is yet another price to be paid, I remind myself that I have to give up to go up.

Going after a dream is like climbing a mountain. We will never make it to the summit if we are carrying too much weight. As we enter each new phase of the climb, we face a decision. Do we take on more things to carry, lay down things that won't help us climb, exchange what we have for something else, or stop climbing altogether? Most people try to take too many things with them on their dream journey. However, when successful people climb, they let go of things or start exchanging them in order to reach a higher level.

After being on my dream journey for more than forty years, I've come to realize that the payments required for reaching a dream never stop. The dream journey continues only if you keep paying the price. The higher you want to go, the more you must give up. And the greater the price you pay, the greater the joy you feel when you finally reach your dream. The greater the investment, the greater the emotional return.

5. It Is Possible to Pay Too Much for Your Dream

While I recognize that every dream has a price, I do not believe that you should be willing to pay *any* price to reach your dream. Some costs are simply too high. For example, I have seen people compromise their values, sacrifice their families, and ruin their health in pursuit of a dream. These are prices I would not be willing to pay.

If you ruin your health or sacrifice your family, even though you achieve your dream, you won't be able to enjoy it. And if you compromise your values, you damage your soul. You cannot allow your dream to dictate your values. Rather, your values should govern your dream. Anytime these two things get out of whack and the dream begins to control your values, the cost is getting too high.

What price is too high to pay for *your* dream? I encourage you to make a list of things that you would protect at all costs. I recommend that you keep it short. Having a long list will probably make it impossible to achieve your dream. Focus on only the essentials, and then be ready and willing to give up everything else.

YOU WILL HAVE TO PAY FOR THESE

I mentioned that every dream is personal, and as a result, the costs will be too. While that is true, I have also found that a few costs are common for all people who pursue dreams. I believe that everyone must pay at least these three in order to succeed.

1. Pay the Price of Dealing with Criticism from People Who Matter

Philosopher-poet Ralph Waldo Emerson spoke about what is required to stay on track: "Whatever course you decide upon, there is always someone to tell you that you are wrong. There are always difficulties arising which tempt you to believe that your critics are right. To map out a course of action and follow it to an end requires courage."

> "*Whatever course you decide upon, there is always someone to tell you that you are wrong. There are always difficulties arising which tempt you to believe that your critics are right. To map out a course of action and follow it to an end requires courage.*"
> —Ralph Waldo Emerson

Everyone who pursues a dream is criticized. If you're thick-skinned, most of it won't bother you. You have to learn to ignore it, just as professional athletes do. They deal with it all the time. For example, it's said that every baseball team could use someone who knows how to play every position, never strikes out, and never makes an error. The only problem is that it's hard to make him lay down his hot dog and come out of the stands!

I think it's human nature for people to criticize others. Jonas Salk, who developed the polio vaccine, said, "First people will tell you that you are wrong. Then they will tell you that you are right, but what you're doing really isn't important. Finally, they will admit that you are right and that what you are doing is very important; but after all, they knew it all the time."

What really hurts is the criticism of people who are important to you. It's hard to have your dream criticized by people you admire, love, and respect. But if you want to achieve your dream, you'll have to learn how to pay that price too. Stacy Allison, the first American woman to reach the summit of Mt. Everest, remarked, "You've got to decide sometimes in your life when it's okay not to listen to what other people are saying. If I had listened to other people I wouldn't have climbed Mt. Everest."

So when should you listen and when should you ignore what others have to say? Which critics count and which don't? Here is my advice. Heed the advice of the critic when . . .

- ⊛ You are unconditionally loved by the one who criticizes you.
- ⊛ The criticism is not tainted by his or her personal agenda.
- ⊛ The person is not naturally critical of everything.
- ⊛ The person will continue giving support after giving advice.
- ⊛ He or she has knowledge and success in the area of the criticism.

Facing criticism is simply one of the prices you will have to pay to achieve your dream. You just can't let it get to you. Author Max Lucado writes about this in his book *He Still Moves Stones*. He quotes Mark 5:36, "But Jesus paid no attention to what they said," and then goes on to say,

> I love that line! It describes the critical principle for seeing the unseen: Ignore what people say. Block them out. Turn them off.

Close your ears. And, if you have to, walk away.

Ignore the ones who say it's too late to start over.

Disregard those who say you'll never amount to anything.

Turn a deaf ear toward those who say that you aren't smart enough, fast enough, tall enough, or big enough—ignore them.

Faith sometimes begins by stuffing your ears with cotton.

Jesus turns immediately to Jairus and pleads: "Don't be afraid, just believe."

Jesus compels Jairus to see the unseen. When Jesus says, "Just believe . . . " He is imploring, "Don't limit your possibilities to the visible. Don't listen only for the audible. Don't be controlled by the logical. Believe there is more to life than meets the eye!"[4]

People who keep pursuing their dreams—even as others express their doubt and criticism—always believe that there is more than meets the eye. It's one of the things that keeps them going.

2. Pay the Price of Overcoming Your Fears

Have you ever wondered how animal trainers can control a five-ton elephant and keep it from running away? They do it by controlling the animal's thinking. When a baby elephant is being trained, a rope is put on its leg and then tied to a wooden post secured in the ground. The elephant, which is not yet very strong, pulls at the rope but is unable to break it or pull up the post. Eventually it gives up. From that point forward, when the elephant's leg is secured, it *believes* it cannot get away—even though it is fully capable of escaping and has been for a long time. It remembers its struggle. That's one reason it's said, "Elephants never forget."

People are like that. Their thinking limits them, just as an elephant's does. Usually it's because of fear. The truth is that fear can steal your dreams. You may be afraid of failure. You may fear rejection. You may not want to make a fool of yourself. You may be afraid of trying because you believe you can't succeed. If you give in to these thoughts and believe that you can't achieve your dream, then you'll be right—and therefore unable to achieve your dream. But here's the good news: fear is common to all of us, and it can be overcome.

Of course, not all fear is bad. Fear can warn us of danger. And our fears that are connected to reality can help us. But when fear is irrational or disproportionate to the threat, it harms us. It keeps us from doing what we can and becoming what we must to achieve our dreams.

Former Surgeon General C. Everett Koop asserted, "People have an inappropriate sense of what is dangerous." What they fear often has no connection to reality. For example, people fear flying, yet they are more likely to choke to death on food than to die on a commercial aircraft. They fear being stabbed to death by a stranger, yet they are twice as likely to be killed playing a sport. They fear being killed by a shark, yet barnyard pigs kill more people than sharks do. People fear dying during a medical procedure, yet they are sixteen times more likely to die in a car accident than from a medical complication.[5]

> *All dreams are outside our comfort zone.*
> *Leaving that zone is a price we must pay to achieve them.*

All dreams are outside our comfort zone. Leaving that zone is a price we must pay to achieve them. In his book *The Success Principles:*

How to Get from Where You Are to Where You Want to Be Jack Canfield writes, "Think of your comfort zone as a prison you live in—a largely self-created prison. It consists of a collection of can'ts, musts, must nots and other unfounded beliefs formed from all the negative thoughts and decisions you have accumulated and reinforced during your lifetime."[6] Every fear is like a bar of that prison. But the good news is that because fears are feelings, the faulty ones can be removed, and we can become free from them. But it costs us to remove them.

> *"Think of your comfort zone as a prison you live in—a largely self-created prison. It consists of a collection of can'ts, musts, must nots and other unfounded beliefs formed from all the negative thoughts and decisions you have accumulated and reinforced during your lifetime."*
> —JACK CANFIELD

Of course, some fears are based on reality. We still need to deal with them. Playwright David Mamet wrote:

On June 5th, 1944 thousands of American paratroopers jumped into Normandy. Four men refused the jump. Can you imagine, can anyone imagine the rest of these men's lives? What prodigies of self-excuse, rationale, or repression they must have had to employ? Their lives, in effect, ended the moment they refused to leave the plane. As would the lives of the Jews, had they refused to go into the sea. As will yours and mine, and as they do in part,

we each refuse the opportunity to change—we stagnate and perform ever greater prodigies of repression and hypocrisy, to
explain to ourselves why we don't immerse ourselves in the mys-
teries of life. We all die in the end, but there's no reason to die in
the middle.[7]

You don't want die in the middle of your life! Nobody does. The
truth is that everyone has to pay one way or another. You can listen
to your fears and pay with your life. Or you can pay the price of
overcoming your fears and live. It's up to you.

It is my desire for you to experience the sweetness of your
dreams, to know what Kevin Myers meant when he said, "It's much
more dangerous and adventurous to dream than most people dare
to believe. But it is a great chase!" To do that, you must develop
courage to face the danger. You must learn to live fearlessly for the
sake of your dream. That's no easy task. Writer and historian Michael
Ignatieff comments:

Living fearlessly is not the same thing as never being afraid. It's
good to be afraid occasionally. Fear is a great teacher. What's not
good is living in fear, allowing fear to dictate your choices, allowing fear to define who you are. Living fearlessly means standing
up to fear, taking its measure, refusing to let it shape and define
your life. Living fearlessly means taking risks, taking gambles,
not playing it safe. It means refusing to take "no" for an answer
when you are sure that the answer should have been "yes." It
means refusing to settle for less than what is your due, what is
yours by right, what is yours by the sweat of your labor and your
effort.[8]

Living fearlessly is a matter of choice. It is the choice that often separates those who pay the price for the dream and achieve it, and those who refuse to pay it and fail. Why? Because you need courage to answer the Cost Question. You have to be fearless to pay the price for your dream.

3. Pay the Price of Hard Work

Recently after I spoke to employees at a company in Denver, an attendee named Rich Melman came up to me and handed me this quote: "It is hard to be 100 percent better than your competition, but you can be 1 percent better in 100 ways." That's the kind of die-hard attitude that is needed to achieve your dream.

> *"It is hard to be 100 percent better than your*
> *competition, but you can be 1 percent better in 100 ways."*
> —Rich Melman

Let's face it: dreams don't work unless you do. When it comes to success, there are no escalators that you can ride to the top. You have to make the climb, and that means hard work. Author and syndicated business columnist Dale Dauten offers this straightforward advice: "If you want to be creative in your company, your career, your life, all it takes is one easy step . . . the extra one. When you encounter a familiar plan, you just ask one question: What else could we do?"

Achieving a dream will require hard work. To succeed, you'll have to do more—more than you may want, more than your competition, more than you think you're capable of. You must live these words of William Arthur Ward:

I will do more than belong—I will participate.

I will do more than care—I will help.

I will do more than believe—I will practice.

I will do more than be fair—I will be kind.

I will do more than forgive—I will forget.

I will do more than dream—I will work.

I will do more than teach—I will inspire.

I will do more than earn—I will enrich.

I will do more than give—I will serve.

I will do more than live—I will grow.

I will do more than suffer—I will triumph.[9]

You can't do whatever's easiest and still realize a dream. You have to do more. You must do whatever it takes.

Though it will cost you a great deal to realize your dream, the rewards are worth the effort. American founding father Thomas Paine wrote in *The American Crisis*, "The harder the conflict, the more glorious the triumph. What we obtain too cheap, we esteem too lightly; it is dearness only that gives every thing its value."

Answering the Cost Question separates the uncommitted from the committed. It takes a lot of courage to let go of something you love. It takes a lot of commitment and work to pay the price for a dream. And even if you do pay the price, there are no guarantees that you will achieve your dream. However, I guarantee you that if you *don't* pay the price, you *will not* achieve it. To be successful, you must take that risk. You must challenge the status quo and get out of your comfort zone. You must give all you have—and then some.

WILLING TO PAY

That's what Terry Fox did. In 1977 when he was eighteen years old, he was diagnosed with bone cancer. As a result, his right leg was amputated. While he was recovering and undergoing chemotherapy, he was struck by how many people were suffering from cancer, particularly children. Inspired by the story of another cancer survivor who ran the New York City Marathon, Fox began running with the aid of a prosthetic leg. Soon he dreamed of doing what seemed impossible: running across the nation of Canada to raise money for cancer research.

He started preparing. He ran more than 3,100 miles during an eighteen-month period to train.[10] Because prosthetics were not very sophisticated in those days, it always cost him. After every training run, his stump would be covered with cysts and bleeding sores. Yet he was undeterred.

On April 12, 1980, Fox started what came to be called the Marathon of Hope on the Atlantic coast near St. John's, Newfoundland. Every day he ran from twenty-four to thirty miles. At first, his efforts received little attention. In early May as he entered Nova Scotia, few people greeted him. In early June, it was much the same. Still, he kept running. When someone asked how he kept himself going with thousands of miles to run still ahead of him, he answered, "I just keep running to the next telephone pole."[11]

But by the end of June, word began to spread about his efforts.

Donations began flowing in. He met Prime Minister Pierre Trudeau. A song was written in Fox's honor. News organizations covered his progress.

Fox ran for 143 days and covered more than 3,300 miles. He was willing to answer the Cost Question. He was willing to pay the price. Then on September 1, 1980, he was forced to stop in Thunder Bay, Ontario, because what he thought was a cold turned out to be more cancer—this time in his lungs.

"People thought I was going through hell," Fox said. "Maybe I was partly, but still I was doing what I wanted and a dream was coming true."[12]

Terry beat cancer the first time when it was in his leg, and he expected to beat it again. At a press conference shortly after he had stopped his long race, Terry said, "How many people do something they really believe in? I just wish people would realize that anything's possible if you try. Dreams are made if people try."[13] He wanted to achieve his dream of finishing the Marathon of Hope. In fact, when members of the Toronto Maple Leafs hockey team offered to finish it for him, he declined. But he never recovered from cancer. Less than a year later, he died.

Terry Fox's indomitable spirit lives on. Although he was unable to finish his race, his dream was realized without him. Even before Terry died, an annual Terry Fox Run was being planned to commemorate his Marathon of Hope and to raise money for cancer research. The first one was held in 1981, attracted 300,000 participants in Canada, and raised $3.5 million. Today an annual run is held in countries around the world. And so far, more than $400 million has been raised worldwide for cancer research through the annual Terry Fox Run.[14]

What are you willing to pay for your dream? Do you have the

courage to answer the Cost Question? Are you willing to live fearlessly, as Terry Fox did? Are you willing to pay the price even if you are uncertain whether it will be enough to buy your dream? I hope your answer is yes.

CAN YOU ANSWER YES TO THE COST QUESTION:
AM I WILLING TO PAY THE PRICE FOR MY DREAM?

What is your dream worth? That is what you need to figure out if you are unsure about your answer to the Cost Question. You need to count the cost.

First, seek out someone with experience in your area of interest. Ask him or her to give you information and advice about what it takes to achieve success in that field.

Next, spend some time thinking about the following questions, and write out your answers:

How much am I willing to pay for my dream?
How soon am I willing to pay it?
How often am I willing to pay it?
How will I handle the criticism I will face?
How will I overcome my fears?
How hard am I willing to work?
What am I *not* willing to pay? (Remember, some prices are too high.)

Don't forget: the bigger the dream, the higher the cost. If you are unwilling to pay what it is likely to cost, you need to change your dream or change what you are willing to pay.

CHAPTER 8

The Tenacity Question
Am I Moving Closer to My Dream?

The mere possession of a vision is not the same as living it, nor can we encourage others with it if we do not, ourselves, understand and follow its truths. . . . To be blessed with visions is not enough . . . we must live them!

–HIGH EAGLE

H. Jackson Brown, author of *Life's Little Instruction Book,* says there are two rules of perseverance: "Rule #1 Take one more step. Rule #2 When you can't take one more step, refer to Rule #1." That's what it takes to achieve a dream: the will to take one more step, even when you're convinced you can't. People who live their dreams refuse to give up, knowing that if they keep chipping away, making whatever small progress they can every day, they increase the chance that something will happen in their favor. They answer yes to the Tenacity Question, which asks, Am I moving closer to my dream?

> *"Rule #1 Take one more step. Rule #2 When you can't take one more step, refer to Rule #1."*
> –H. JACKSON BROWN

A PICTURE OF TENACITY

Study the lives of leaders and entrepreneurs, and you see that all share the quality of tenacity. Despite negative circumstances, obstacles, and injustices, they persevere. They move closer to their dreams day by day.

Recently I learned about the story of Elizabeth Keckly, a model of tenacity. She was born a slave in 1818 in Virginia and soon experienced a life of hardship and abuse. She was made to care for an infant when she was only four years old and was beaten at age five when she tipped over the baby's cradle. She was separated from her father. She was sexually abused. And she was repeatedly told by her owners that she would never be "worth her salt." From an early age, she was painfully aware of the plight of those living in slavery. In her autobiography she wrote:

When I was about seven years old I witnessed, for the first time, the sale of a human being. . . . The master had just purchased his hogs for winter, for which he was unable to pay in full. To escape from his embarrassment it was necessary to sell one of the slaves. Little Joe, the son of the cook, was selected as the victim. His mother was ordered to dress him up in his Sunday clothes, and send him to the house. He came in with a bright face, was placed in the scales, and was sold, like the hogs, at so much per pound. His mother was kept in ignorance of the transaction, but her suspicions were aroused. When her son started for Petersburg in the wagon, the truth began to dawn upon her mind, and she pleaded piteously that her boy should not be taken from her; but master quieted her by telling her that he was simply going to town with the wagon, and would be back in the morning. Morning came, but little Joe did not return to his mother. Morning after morning passed, and the mother went down to the grave without ever seeing her child again. One day she was whipped for grieving [for] her lost boy. Colonel Burwell [their owner] never liked to see one of his slaves wear a sorrowful face.[1]

Keckly had a tough life, which she described as having gone to "the hardy school." She gave birth to a child after being raped by a white man. She was often required to do the work of three people. But she also was highly tenacious and made the most of her opportunities. She learned to read and write. She developed skill as a seamstress, having learned beginning at age six from her mother. And she developed a mind for business, which she ultimately used to change her life.

DREAMS OF FREEDOM

Keckly grew up in a rural area. However, when the family she served moved to the town of Petersburg, Virginia, something important happened: Keckly, who was in her midtwenties, saw the potential of becoming an entrepreneur. About half of the population of Petersburg was black, and about a third of those blacks were free.[2] As she traveled around town, she discovered that many free blacks were single women who owned property and ran their own businesses. Keckly saw possibilities for herself because by then she had developed into a dressmaker of the highest caliber.

A dream began to plant its seed within her. Ever the pragmatist, up to that time Keckly had always made the best of her life as a slave, overcoming abuse, working hard, and living with integrity. Now, for the first time, she considered the possibility that someday she might gain her freedom and work for herself. Harvard professor Jennifer Fleischner observes, "In these working- and middle-class black women Lizzy could see the possibilities beyond slavery for someone like her. With the taste of autonomy new in her mouth—never before had she had so much freedom of movement or of thought as here in Petersburg—she began hungering for more."[3]

Another relocation—this time to St. Louis, Missouri, when she was twenty-nine years old—made the dream within Keckly grow even stronger. The family she served was experiencing hard times, so to earn money she began making dresses not only for the women of that family, but also for other prominent society ladies in town.

"With my needle," Keckly recalled, "I kept bread in the mouths of seventeen persons for two years and five months."[4] More and more, independence—both legal and economic—was on her mind.

When she broached the subject with her owner of buying her freedom, he refused to discuss it and ordered her never to bring it up again. But by then the dream was too important, and she would not give up. The same spirit of tenacity that had helped her to survive hardship became focused on her desire to buy freedom for herself and her son. "I would not be put off thus," Keckly noted, "for hope pointed to a freer, brighter life in the future."[5] Once when she brought up the subject, her owner offered her a silver quarter and told her to take the ferry across the river to Illinois, a free state. He was suggesting she run away. She refused.

"By the laws of the land I am your slave—you are my master," she told her owner, "and I will only be free by such means as the laws of my country provide."[6]

Finally when the family's financial situation became desperate, her owner named a price: $1,200. It was a huge amount, probably the equivalent today of about $25,000. But that didn't stop Keckly. No matter what amount her owner had named, she would have found a way to pay it. No price for a dream is too great for someone with her tenacity.

Initially she planned to travel to New York to ask a charitable organization to lend her the money. But much to her surprise, the women for whom she had been making dresses came to her aid, each giving her what she could.

On November 13, 1855, Elizabeth Keckly bought freedom for her son and herself. In her autobiography she wrote,

> The twelve hundred dollars were raised, and at last my son and myself were free. Free, free! What a glorious ring to the word. Free! the bitter heart-struggle was over. Free! the soul could go out to heaven and to God with no chains to clog its flight or pull it down. Free! the earth wore a brighter look, and the very stars seemed to sing with joy. Yes, free! free by the laws of man and the smile of God—and Heaven bless them who made me so![7]

Though the money was offered as a gift, Keckly accepted it only as a loan. She worked diligently for five years in St. Louis and paid back every cent.

A CAREER BEYOND SLAVERY

Freedom was only half of Keckly's dream. The other half was to be a successful businessperson. To realize it, she moved first to

Baltimore and then to Washington, D.C., where she began working as a dressmaker. Due to her exceptional sewing skills, her ability as a networker, and the sterling recommendations she received from her St. Louis clients, she soon had all the work she could handle. She was actually succeeding! And then an even loftier dream became clear in her mind.

"Ever since arriving in Washington," Keckly explained, "I had a great desire to work for the ladies of the White House, and to accomplish this end I was ready to make almost any sacrifice consistent with propriety."[8] There was no more visible person in the United States for whom she could make dresses than the first lady. She continued working, making the most of word-of-mouth referrals. Within a year, she achieved her goal. Keckly became the exclusive dressmaker, fashion consultant, and sometimes dresser for Mary Todd Lincoln starting the day after Abraham Lincoln's inauguration. She also became Mrs. Lincoln's closest friend and confidante. Keckly consoled Lincoln when her son Willie died. And after the president was assassinated, when she was asked, "Is there no one, Mrs. Lincoln, that you desire to have with you in this terrible affliction?" the first lady replied, "Yes, send for Elizabeth Keckly."[9] Lincoln was much comforted by her. For years after the president's death, she often described Keckly as her best friend.[10]

Keckly's business flourished in Washington. At one point she was so busy that she opened a second shop. In her later years, she became known as a teacher of sewing. She did all that she had dreamed of—and much more than others thought she was capable of. And she took great delight in the fact that in the years following the Civil War, she had done better and was better off financially than the children of her former owners.[11] If anyone had asked her the

Cost Question—Am I willing to pay the price for my dream?—no doubt she would have answered a resounding yes.

DOES YOUR DREAM MAKE YOU STRONGER OR WEAKER?

What about you? How do you answer the Tenacity Question? Are you moving closer to your dream? Are you taking steps forward? Do you have the tenacity to carry you through? Or when things get tough—and they certainly will—are you more likely to give up? Ralph Waldo Emerson observed, "The great majority of men are bundles of beginnings." Are you merely a starter, or are you also a finisher, as Keckly was? When the enthusiasm for a new idea fades, when the passion cools, when the odds against you increase and the results diminish, when it looks as if success is impossible, will you maintain your intensity and keep going? Are you tenacious? That is the mark of people who actually achieve their dream.

> "*The great majority of men are bundles of beginnings.*"
> —RALPH WALDO EMERSON

Calvin Coolidge, the thirtieth president of the United States, asserted, "Persistence and determination alone are omnipotent. The slogan 'press on' has solved and always will solve the problems of the human race." Tenacity is the solution to many a problem that you will encounter on the road to your dream. Consider the fact that Admiral

Robert Peary attempted to reach the North Pole seven times before he finally succeeded. Oscar Hammerstein produced five shows on Broadway that were flops before staging *Oklahoma,* which was seen by more than 4.5 million people during a record breaking run of 2,212 performances. Thomas Edison failed in his attempt to create a workable lightbulb ten thousand times before creating one that finally worked. To achieve your dream, you will have to develop the ability to keep going when others quit. You need to develop tenacity!

KEEP FIGHTING FOR YOUR DREAM

President Woodrow Wilson affirmed the importance of dreams: "We grow by dreams. All big [individuals] are dreamers. They see things in the soft haze of a spring day, or in the red fire on a long winter's evening. Some of us let those great dreams die, but others nourish and protect them; nourish them through bad days until they bring them to the sunshine and light which comes always to those who sincerely hope that their dreams will come true." If you want to become someone who nourishes a dream until it comes true, then you need to keep working, keep striving, keep moving closer to your dream. To do that, keep in mind the following:

1. TO MOVE CLOSER TO YOUR DREAM . . . RECOGNIZE
   THAT QUITTING IS MORE ABOUT WHO YOU ARE
   THAN WHERE YOU ARE

Everyone faces difficulty when working toward a dream. And if someone fails, he can make excuses for what went wrong, how the unexpected happened, how someone let him down, how circumstances worked against him. But the reality is that the external things do not stop people. It's what happens to them on the inside. Most people stop themselves from reaching their potential. They can pretend that people, things, and situations outside themselves are to blame for their failures, but in reality, they are to blame.

Most people stop themselves from reaching their potential.

People who achieve their dreams don't have an easier path than those who do not. Think of Elizabeth Keckly. Just about everything was working against her, yet she succeeded in achieving her dreams. We shouldn't make excuses. Instead our attitude should be like that of the gifted artist and inventor Leonardo da Vinci, who declared, "Obstacles cannot crush me. Every obstacle yields to stern resolve. He who is fixed on a star does not change his mind." One must have that mind-set to tenaciously pursue a dream. The only guarantee for failure is to stop trying. There is no insurmountable barrier except our inherent lack of persistence.

There is a legend about a soldier who was court-martialed before Alexander the Great. Feeling the verdict was unjust, the soldier asked to appeal it. The conqueror informed the soldier there was no one higher than him to whom he could plead his case. "In that case," the soldier replied, "I appeal my case from Alexander the Small to Alexander the Great."

The story is probably apocryphal, yet it points to a truth we must face. In each of us there are a lower self and a greater self struggling for supremacy. The lower one leads us to defeat, the greater to victory. Here's what I mean:

Our lower self says, "Not enough people
believe in you. You'll never make it."

Our greater self says, "My belief in
myself is enough; I can make it."

The only guarantee for failure is to stop trying.

Tawni O'Dell, the author of *Back Roads*, an Oprah Book Club pick, heeded her greater self when she remarked, "Never give up on your dream. . . . Perseverance is all important. If you don't have the desire and the belief in yourself to keep trying after you've been told you should quit, you'll never make it."[12]

Our lower self says, "It's taking too
long to realize your dream."

Our greater self says, "Dreams are
realized one day at a time."

The diary of Christopher Columbus shows that he fed the greater self and starved the lower as he went through rough storms, dealt with damaged ships, faced deprivation, and feared mutiny. Day after day, the entries in his log were alike: "This day we sailed on."

Our lower self says, "Enough is enough!
You've taken enough hits."

Our greater self says, "I've come
too far to give up now."

Writer H. E. Jensen must have been listening to his greater self when he said, "The man who wins may have been counted out several times, but he didn't hear the referee."

Our lower self says, "You don't have the
strength to hold on to your dream."

Our greater self says, "Hold on a little longer;
the darkest hour is just before the dawn."

Novelist Harriet Beecher Stowe obeyed her greater self and said, "When you get into a tight place and everything goes against you, till it seems as though you could not hang on a minute longer, never give up then, for that is just the place and time that the tide will turn."

> *"The man who wins may have been counted out*
> *several times, but he didn't hear the referee."*
> —H. E. JENSEN

So when things go wrong, when the obstacles seem too great, when the difficulties get to be too much, when your dream seems to be impossibly far away, your job is to simply keep going. If you stop, it won't be because of what happens around you. It will be because of what happens within you. Success is probably closer than you think. Just keep moving forward.

2. To Move Closer to Your Dream...
Improve Your Vocabulary

During the early 1970s when I was trying to work through difficult leadership issues, months went by, and still I could find no answers. I felt like throwing in the towel. But I am not a quitter by nature—I hate losing too much. One day in exasperation I pulled out a dictionary and looked at the word *quit*. I read the definition and spent a few minutes considering that option. I just couldn't do it. In a symbolic act of defiance, I took my scissors and cut the word right out of my dictionary—and out of my vocabulary. I would do whatever it took to succeed. That decision didn't make any of my problems go away, but it sure did strengthen my resolve.

If you want to achieve your dream, you need to pay attention to what you say. French novelist Emile de Girardin noted the power of words: "The power of words is immense. Well chosen words have stopped armies, changed defeat into victory, and saved empires." The words you use have the power to move you closer to or farther away from your dream. Take a look at the difference between the following statements:

Can't	Can Do
We've never done it before.	We have the opportunity to be first.
We don't have the resources.	Necessity fuels invention.

There's not enough time.	We'll change how we work.
We already tried that.	We learned from the experience.
It's a waste of time.	Think of the possibilities.
We don't have the expertise.	Let's network with those who do.
Our vendors won't go for it.	Let's show them the opportunities.
We don't have enough money.	Maybe there's something we can cut.
We're understaffed.	We're a lean, hungry team.
We don't have the equipment.	Maybe we can sub it out.
It'll never get any better.	We'll try one more time.
Let somebody else deal with it.	I'm ready to learn something new.
It's too radical.	Let's take a chance.
Our customers won't buy it.	They love it when they understand it.
It's not my job.	I'll be glad to take the responsibility.
I can't!	Yes, I can!

If you hear yourself saying that you can't do something, then you will be unable to do it—even if you have the talent, time, resources, strategy, and people to accomplish it. Only those who say they can, do. Saying you believe in yourself will not guarantee your success, but saying you *don't* believe in yourself will guarantee your failure.

> *Saying you believe in yourself will not guarantee your success, but saying you don't believe in yourself will guarantee your failure.*

I love the perspective of Bill Boeing, who founded Boeing Aircraft in 1916. On plaque at the company's former headquarters is a quote by him, which says, "It behooves no one to dismiss any novel idea with the statement that it 'can't be done.' Our job is to keep everlastingly at research and experiment, to adapt our laboratories to production as soon as practicable, to let no new improvement in flying and flying equipment pass us by." That attitude has kept his dream and the Boeing company alive for more than ninety years!

3. TO MOVE CLOSER TO YOUR DREAM . . . RECOGNIZE THAT WAITING FOR EVERYTHING TO BE RIGHT IS WRONG

Comedian Jonathan Winters advised, "If your ship doesn't come in, swim out to meet it." Too many people stand on the dock waiting. They want the ship in place, the gangplank perfectly positioned, the weather right, and an engraved invitation before they're willing to take a step forward! It will never happen. Why? Because our dreams don't move toward us. We have to move toward them.

> *"If your ship doesn't come in, swim out to meet it."*
> —JONATHAN WINTERS

Jack Canfield, in his wonderful book *The Success Principles: How to Get from Where You Are to Where You Want to Be*, writes:

It's time to quit waiting for
Perfection
Inspiration

Permission

Reassurance

Someone to change

The right person to come along

The kids to leave home

A more favorable horoscope

The new administration to take over

An absence of risk

Someone to discover you

A clear set of instructions

More self-confidence

The pain to go away[13]

In other words, the conditions will never be perfect for you to go after your dream. In fact, conditions may not seem all that favorable. Move forward anyway. Be tenacious in your commitment to action.

4. To Move Closer to Your Dream . . . Change Your Thinking

If you compare the thinking of people who give up easily versus people who tenaciously move forward in pursuit of their dreams, do you know what one of the main differences would be? Believe it or not, successful people don't spend the majority of their time thinking about what must be done. Instead, they spend about twice as much time reflecting on what they have already accomplished and on how they are capable of accomplishing what they set out to do.

I love the way retired UCLA basketball coach John Wooden expresses this idea: "Things turn out best for the people who make the best of the way things turn out." Successful people are positive. They believe they can get things done. For the most part, they enjoy what they're doing. And those things are important because pursuing a dream is a bumpy journey. It is uphill. It has a lot of dead ends. Only those who think right succeed.

> *"Things turn out best for the people who make the best of the way things turn out."*
> —JOHN WOODEN

The greatest gap between successful and unsuccessful people is the thinking gap. Successful people think differently from unsuccessful people, especially in the area of failure. They see it as a regular part of success, and they get over it. Jonas Salk, physician, research scientist, and developer of the polio vaccine, observed:

As I look upon the experience of an experimentalist, everything that you do is, in a sense, succeeding. It's telling you what not to do, as well as what to do. Not infrequently, I go into the laboratory, and people would say something didn't work. And I say, "Great, we've made a great discovery!" If you thought it was going to work, and it didn't work, that tells you as much as if it did. So my attitude is not one of pitfalls; my attitude is one of challenges and "What is nature telling me?"[14]

That tenacity comes from right thinking. And it is the hallmark of successful people. They keep trying, keep learning, keep moving forward. They win the battle in their minds, and then it overflows into what they do. They display the same kind of attitude that inventor Thomas Edison did as he stated, "When I have fully decided that a result is worth getting, I go ahead on it and make trial after trial until it comes." If you want to keep moving toward your dream, you need a similar attitude.

5. To Move Closer to Your Dream . . . Recognize That the Resources for Your Dream Stop the Moment You Do

There is a strong relationship between our movement toward our dreams and the resources we need becoming available to us. Too often we want to see the resources or have them in hand before we start moving forward. But when we do that, we have neither resources nor movement. Instead, we need to be like the snail in a humorous story as he started climbing an apple tree one cold day in February. As he inched his way upward, a worm stuck his head out from a crevice in the tree and said, "You're wasting your energy. There isn't a single apple up there."

"No," replied the snail as he kept climbing, "but there will be when I get there!"[15] The story is corny, but the sentiment is true. Only by moving forward will we have an opportunity to receive what we need to succeed.

In 1995, my brother Larry and I founded EQUIP, a nonprofit organization that has trained more than two million leaders around the world. At an event at Pebble Beach that celebrated the organization's tenth anniversary, I had the opportunity to speak to three hundred of EQUIP's donors. As I looked into the faces of the men and women who were financially committed to the dream of training leaders internationally, I realized that I knew only about twenty-five of them when EQUIP was born. More than 90 percent of these key people—and the resources they provide—came into the picture *after* we started moving forward. We didn't launch EQUIP because we already *had* the resources we needed. We launched EQUIP because we *needed* those resources.

> *"Effort only releases its reward after a person refuses to quit."*
> —W. CLEMENT STONE

That's the way it always works. Vision doesn't follow resources. It happens the other way around. First we have the dream. Then we have to move forward. Then—and only then—do people and resources follow. As businessman and author W. Clement Stone said, "Effort only releases its reward after a person refuses to quit."

6. TO MOVE CLOSER TO YOUR DREAM . . . PRACTICE THE RULE OF FIVE

Millions of people, including me, have been inspired by the stories in Mark Victor Hansen and Jack Canfield's Chicken Soup for the Soul books. I think most people would assume that publishers were breaking down their doors for the opportunity to get those books to market. Not a chance. It was a huge struggle. Hansen and Canfield had a very difficult time getting anyone interested in publishing the first book. Then, when the book was in print, they had a tough time getting anyone to buy it. They did a lot of research and talked to a lot of successful authors. But what finally helped them turn the corner was advice from a teacher named Scolastico, who told them, "If you would go every day to a very large tree and take five swings at it with a very sharp ax, eventually, no matter how large the tree, it would have to come down."

From that advice, the authors developed what they call the "rule of five." Every day they did five specific things that would move them closer to their dream of selling books. They write:

> With the goal of getting *Chicken Soup for the Soul* to the top of the *New York Times* Best-Seller List, it meant having five radio interviews or sending out five review copies to editors who might review the book or calling five network marketing companies and asking them to buy the book as a motivational tool for their salespeople or giving a seminar to at least five people and selling the book in the back of the room. On some days we would simply send out five free copies to people listed in the *Celebrity Address Book*—people such as Harrison Ford, Barbra Streisand, Paul McCartney, Steven Spielberg, and Sidney Poitier. As a result of that one activity, I ended up meeting Sidney Poitier—at his request—and we later learned that the producer of the television show *Touched by an Angel* required all of the people working on the show to read *Chicken Soup for the Soul* to put them in "the right frame of mind." One day we sent copies of the book to all the jurors in the O. J. Simpson trial. A week later, we received a nice letter from Judge Lance Ito thanking us for thinking of the jurors, who were sequestered and not allowed to watch television or read the newspapers. The next day, four of the jurors were spotted reading the book by the press, and that led to some valuable public relations for the book.

We made phone calls to people who could review the book, we wrote press releases, we called in to talk shows (some at 3 am), we gave away free copies at our talks, we sent them to ministers to use as a source of talks for their sermons, we gave free "Chicken Soup for the Soul" talks at churches, we did book signings at any bookstore that would have us, we asked businesses to make bulk purchases for their employees, we got the book into the PXs on military bases, we asked our fellow speakers to sell the books at their talks, we asked seminar companies to put it in their catalogues, we bought a directory of catalogues and asked all the appropriate ones to carry the book, we visited gift shops and card shops and asked them to carry the book—we even got gas stations, bakeries, and restaurants to sell the book. It was a lot of effort—a minimum of five things a day, every day, day in and day out—for over two years.[16]

Was using the rule of five effective? You be the judge. The *Chicken Soup for the Soul* franchise has 170 titles published in forty-one languages and has sold 112 million copies.[17] If you can have a similar kind of tenacity and consistency for that duration, I bet you'll see great progress toward your dream too!

7. TO MOVE CLOSER TO YOUR DREAM . . . REMEMBER THAT WHEN YOU HAVE EXHAUSTED ALL POSSIBILITIES—YOU HAVEN'T

Many years ago, I had an executive assistant named Barbara Brumagin. Like my current longtime assistant, Linda Eggers, Barbara was excellent. I will always be indebted to her for the service she gave me during those years. But I clearly remember a turning point in her performance in our early working relationship. It occurred the day that she developed a tenacity that set her apart from most of the people I've worked with over the years.

Barbara had been my assistant only a few weeks when I asked her to find a phone number for someone I needed to call. Within a few minutes, Barbara returned to my office and told me that she couldn't find the number. This was in the early 1980s, before the Internet made such tasks simpler.

"Barbara, that's not acceptable," I said, realizing that the nature of our working relationship was going to be impacted by what happened in the next few minutes. "Bring me your Rolodex; then sit down next to me."

I flipped through the phone numbers in the Rolodex, looking for a starting point. Then I began making calls. I followed the trail wherever it led, jotting down notes and numbers as I went. It was no easy task, but finally after about forty-five minutes, I found the number I had asked her for. Then I handed it to her and said, "Barbara, there is always a way to find an answer. It's your job to finish the task. Let's not have this conversation again." And guess what? We never did. I may not have always gotten everything as quickly as I wanted, but Barbara never gave up.

If you want to reach your dream, you can't give up. Even if every avenue looks like a dead end and you feel that you've exhausted every possibility, you haven't. There are always other ways, other options, other opportunities. Even if you don't see them right now, they are there. Don't give up.

Former heavyweight champion Jack Dempsey said, "A champion is one who gets up when he can't." I believe people who achieve their dreams keep going when they think they can't. They are tenaciously persistent. As a result, they keep moving closer to their dreams day by day. Some days they may be moving only a few inches at a time, but they are moving forward.

"A champion is one who gets up when he can't."
—JACK DEMPSEY

A dream is not only a vision that compels you to follow it forward into the future; it is also a measuring tool for every day and a motivation for every effort. If you have chosen your dream wisely, then you must pursue it tenaciously.

CAN YOU ANSWER YES TO THE TENACITY QUESTION: AM I MOVING CLOSER TO MY DREAM?

If you are not moving closer to your dream, then you may not be tenacious enough in your pursuit of it. The key to developing greater tenacity is to change, not to work harder at the same things. Consider which of the things mentioned in the chapter you need to focus on:

Change your thinking. Are you convinced that you can't succeed? Do you describe yourself or what you're doing in negative terms? Are you afraid to get started because conditions aren't favorable? Do you stop trying to move forward when you don't have the resources you need? If so, you need to change your mind-set. What can you do differently today to break the cycle of negative thinking?

Change your perspective. Do you have a short-term mind-set about achieving your dream? Are you expecting success in days, weeks, or months? Remember, the bigger the dream, the longer it is likely to take. Recalibrate your expectations. Create a more reasonable timetable for achieving your dream.

Change your work habits. Adopt the rule of five. What five things can you do today to advance your cause and bring you closer to your dream—no matter how small the progress? Don't forget that what author and publisher Robert Collier says is true: "Success is the sum of small efforts, repeated day in and day out."

CHAPTER 9

The Fulfillment Question
Does Working toward My Dream
Bring Satisfaction?

If one advances confidently in the direction of his dreams,
and endeavors to live the life which he has imagined,
he will meet with a success unexpected in common hours.

—HENRY DAVID THOREAU[1]

If you are passionate about your dream, you probably have the energy and incentive it takes to get moving and take steps to pursue it. If you have answered the Cost Question positively, then you are ready to make sacrifices to see your dream come to fruition. If you possess tenacity, then you probably won't give up on your dream if the pursuit of it becomes difficult. Are these qualities enough to carry you through? Maybe. But there's another question that must be asked, one that speaks to whether the dream you are pursuing is worth all the effort, time, and attention you are giving to it. You must answer the Fulfillment Question: Does working toward my dream bring satisfaction?

"Does that really matter?" you may be asking. "What's the difference as long as I achieve the dream without violating my values?"

> *Achieving a dream is about more than just what you accomplish. It's about who you become in the process!*

I believe it makes all the difference because achieving a dream is about more than just what you accomplish. It's about who you become in the process! A great dream isn't merely a destination. It's the catalyst for a great journey. If that journey is right and you can answer yes to the Fulfillment Question, I wouldn't go so far as to say that the destination doesn't matter, but I will say that if you don't actually reach your dream, the journey is still worth taking. Why? Because the journey itself is fulfilling.

FULFILLMENT OR FRUSTRATION?

There is always a huge gap between the birth of a dream and the achievement of that dream. The question you have to ask yourself is whether it will be a fulfillment gap or a frustration gap. If it's a frustration gap, you will be miserable most of the days you're in it. And every day that you are frustrated instead of fulfilled, you lessen the odds that you will be able to keep moving toward your dream.

Author and marketing expert Seth Godin calls this gap between when you set out to do something and when you actually start to see significant results "the dip," and he has written a book about it. He says that every person should try to be the best in the world at what he does. He believes that is the only way to succeed. (He argues that anything we might be doing that doesn't have the potential to lead to such heights is a cul-de-sac—a dead end—and should be abandoned.) But to become the best, we must first go through the dip, which looks like: "a valley followed by a steep, tall peak. That metaphorical peak is what a person mut climb if he is to become really great at something."

Says Godin, "All our successes are the same. All our failures, too. We succeed when we do something remarkable. We fail when we give up too soon. We succeed when we are the best in the world at what we do. We fail when we get distracted by tasks we don't have the guts to quit."[1] The greater the dip, argues Godin, the greater potential for rewards because the dip weeds out others who might be trying to take the same pathway. I would say that the dip represents both the adversity one must face and the learning curve one must overcome to achieve the desired results. To reach our dreams, we have to go through the gap between conception and realization. That means overcoming obstacles, dealing with difficult learning curves, and doing plain hard work. If we don't have a strong sense of fulfillment that brings us satisfaction along the way, we're going to be in trouble.

FROM WALL STREET TO THE BACK ROADS OF AFRICA

I'm always intrigued when I read about someone who leaves a successful career to follow her dream. Recently I saw profiles in *Fortune* and *Forbes* of someone who fits that description. Her name is Jacqueline Novogratz, and she walked away from a successful and potentially highly lucrative career on Wall Street to pursue something she finds much more fulfilling.

Novogratz has an aptitude for business. The oldest of seven

siblings, she worked her way through college and then took a job in international banking with Chase Manhattan Bank. I guess you could say that business and finance are in the blood in her family. Three of her siblings took a similar path and now enjoy high-profile careers in finance. One is her brother Mike, the president of Fortress Investment Group, who was on *Forbes*' list of the world's richest billionaires in 2007.[2]

Jacqueline Novogratz names Henry Ford as one of her business heroes because he "saw the link between business and consumers—he understood that his workers were also his target market, and he created jobs that lifted wages and he built products that workers could afford."[3]

But besides having a head for finance, Novogratz has a heart for people. She has always possessed a strong desire to help others who are less fortunate. She cites as another of her heroes Indian leader Mahatma Gandhi because he "understood the importance of human equality and human dignity." She also admires what she calls "his brilliance as a marketer and communicator. Through symbolism and words, he was able to move a continent and then the world."[4]

For three years Novogratz traveled the world for Chase Manhattan Bank. She visited forty countries in that time. But while she was in Brazil, the country was going though its debt crisis, and it really impacted her. "I saw all these people in the slums with no access to bank credit at all, while we were writing off millions of dollars of loans to the wealthy," she says. "There was something wrong with this picture."[5] She quit her job and set off in a new direction. She wanted to help the poorest of the poor around the world.

Novogratz recalls arriving on the Ivory Coast as a young,

idealistic woman: "I had just left Wall Street, cut my hair to look like Margaret Mead, given away almost everything I owned, and arrived with all the essentials—some poetry, a few clothes, and, of course, a guitar—because I was going to save the world, and I thought I would just start with the African continent."[6] Needless to say, she was a bit naïve. But she did become involved in something that combined her two loves of helping people and business: microfinance projects. She heard about a bakery run by twenty prostitutes in Kigali, Rwanda. When she went to investigate, what she found instead was a group of unwed mothers who were being supported by a church and being kept busy in a bakery, which was losing money. She determined to help them turn it into a viable business, and in time, she did. The women went from receiving fifty cents a day in charity to earning three times the national average each day in wages.

When she was working on Wall Street, Novogratz says she saw "the power of capital to create businesses and the power of business to create change."[7] As she gained more experience, her vision became clearer. She wanted to combine the power and sustainability of business with a charitable organization's desire to help the poorest of the poor. She attended Stanford and obtained an MBA. Then in 2001 she launched Acumen Fund. According to its Web site,

Acumen Fund is a non-profit global venture fund that uses entrepreneurial approaches to solve the problems of global poverty. We seek to prove that small amounts of philanthropic capital, combined with large doses of business acumen, can build thriving enterprises that serve vast numbers of the poor. Our investments focus on delivering affordable, critical goods and services—like health, water, housing and energy—through innovative, market-oriented approaches.[8]

Novogratz had seen that charitable organizations alone didn't solve problems for poor people because they did not provide long-term solutions. Businesses alone didn't help the poorest people because they looked for rapid gains on investment and did not target the poor. Says Novogratz, "Market-based approaches that support sustainable businesses with the potential to grow when charitable dollars run out can empower people living in poverty to solve their own problems over the long term. Our goal is to transform how the world sees poor people—not as passive recipients of charity, but as individuals with the potential to take control of their own destinies."[9]

Many charitable organzations are helping people in developing countries using microfinance where, for example, they loan women $150 to buy sewing machines. Acumen takes a different approach. It invests $600,000 to $1 million in businesses that provide products and services to the poor in countries such as Egypt, India, Kenya, Pakistan, and Tanzania while creating jobs in those countries at the same time. So far, Acumen has made $27 million in investments in eighteen businesses across Asia and Africa. The investments have contributed to businesses as diverse as medical services in Mumbai, chemical treatment of bed nets in Tanzania to protect against malaria, affordable housing in Pakistan, and drip irrigation systems to small farmers in India.

When Novogratz began working in Africa, she thought she would quickly change the world. Now after twenty years of experience, she is no longer naive, but she remains passionate about what she does. Clearly the work is fulfilling to her. "Even though it is just the beginning," she says, "the thrill of real scalable change is what's extraordinary. And so we can't fool around with one hundred and two hundred. We need to be working on changing the lives of millions of people. And I think we can do it—as a world."[10]

FINDING FULFILLMENT IN THE GAP

If you want the pursuit of your dream to be sustainable, it needs to bring you satisfaction. You must be able to answer the Fulfillment Question with a resounding yes, just as Jacqueline Novogratz has. How does one do that? By learning things that other fulfilled people know as they live in the gap between the birth of a dream and its eventual fruition. Here they are:

1. Fulfilled People Understand the Difference between the Dream and Its Realization

If you have answered the Reality Question positively, then your dream is achievable. However, the ideal picture of your dream that you have in your head is not. It is vital that you understand this if you want to be fulfilled while striving for your dream. If you don't, you're destined for frustration.

Recently I listened to a message on CD by speaker and consultant Dan Sullivan in which he described the difference between our "ideals" and our "actuals." He describes the ideal as "a 'mental construct'—a tool of our brain—that enables us to come to grips with the future. The ideal is a picture that we create of future desirable events and situations that enables us to move forward in time. The ideal does not actually exist outside of our minds, nor is it achievable."[11]

Why isn't the ideal image of your dream achievable? Because it depends on everything's being perfect, and that's not possible. Life is, at best, messy. It's filled with surprises—both good and bad. If you need the ideal picture of your dream to come into being in order to be fulfilled, then you will *never* be fulfilled. You will be forever disappointed.

That doesn't mean you should cast aside your ideal vision. It is useful for helping you to establish goals, find internal motivation, and strive for excellence. However, you also need to temper it. Where idealistic dreams expect to be realized immediately, realistic dreams make you appreciate the time it takes for them to become reality. Where idealistic dreams do not tolerate anything less than perfection, realistic dreams leave room for you to be human and imperfect. Where idealistic dreams set you up for disappointment, realistic dreams set you up for success.

2. FULFILLED PEOPLE UNDERSTAND THAT THE SIZE OF THE DREAM DETERMINES THE SIZE OF THE GAP

The bigger the dream, potentially the more fulfilling it is. However, the bigger the dream, the greater the gap between birth and fruition. If you've chosen a big, hairy, audacious goal (what Jim Collins calls a BHAG), you're going to have to live in a big, hairy, audacious gap. If you've selected a MOAG—mother of all goals—then you can expect the mother of all gaps! That's just the way it is. The larger the plane, the longer the runway; the bigger the goal, the greater the gap.

Andrew Carnegie, the richest man in America during the early 1900s, asserted, "If you want to be happy, set a goal that commands your thoughts, liberates your energy and inspires your hopes." Although that's good advice, you need to keep in mind that you're also setting yourself up for a long distance to travel. And that kind of journey wears out many people. If you want to make the trip, you'll need resolve to keep you going, creativity to overcome obstacles, and other people to help you carry the load.

> *"If you want to be happy, set a goal that commands your thoughts, liberates your energy and inspires your hopes."*
> —ANDREW CARNEGIE

3. FULFILLED PEOPLE KEEP DREAMING WHILE MAKING THE JOURNEY

To keep our dreams alive and to find fulfillment in the pursuit of them, we must allow ourselves to continue dreaming. It is such an essential part of human existence that it has the capacity to keep us going. When Nobel Prize–winning author John Steinbeck was working on *East of Eden,* he wrote to his editor:

I am going to set down Adam's plans for his life. The fact that he isn't going to get even one of them has no emphasis whatever. Plans are real things and not experience. A rich life is rich in plans. If they don't come off, they are still a little bit realized. If they do, they may be disappointing. That's why a trip described becomes better the greater the time between the trip and the telling. I believe too that if you can know a man's plans, you know more about him than you can in any other way. Plans are daydreaming and this is an absolute measure of a man. Thus if I dwell heavily on plans, it is because I am trying to put down the whole man. What a strange life it is. Inspecting it for greatness. There are strange things in people. I guess one of the things that sets us apart from other animals is our dreams and our plans.[12]

I think most creative people intuitively understand the importance of dreaming as a process for inspiration, motivation, and fulfillment. George Lucas, the creator and producer of the Star Wars movies, says that one thing that kept him and his colleagues going during the difficult times was this: "We were always dreaming of how it was going to be." If you are not a naturally creative person, then you may have to learn how to keep dreaming. And if you can do it with a sense of humor, that doesn't hurt. Someone told me that he saw a student riding a bicycle on a college campus. On the student's T-shirt there was the message: "I am going to be a doctor." On his bike was a sign that also had a message: "I am going to be a Mercedes." That's someone who has learned to keep dreaming.

4. FULFILLED PEOPLE APPRECIATE EACH STEP FORWARD IN THE JOURNEY

I have a friend whose answer to me is always the same when I ask how he is doing. "I'm living the dream," he says. Does that mean he has already achieved his dream? No. What he's saying is that his answer to the Fulfillment Question is yes. Just working toward his dream brings satisfaction!

Author and speaker Jim Rohn points out, "The twin killers of success are impatience and greed." I believe they are often the killers of dreams as well. Most people want results that are quick and dramatic. However, the reality is that most dreams are achieved very slowly, and the results come about unspectacularly. If you have achieved any major goals in your life, then you already know that realizing goals can be less thrilling than imagining them. That's why you need to learn to take satisfaction in the journey and find fulfillment in the small steps along the way. Aviation pioneer Amelia Earhart asserted, "You can do anything you decide to do. You can act to change and control your life; and the procedure, the process is its own reward."

> *"The twin killers of success are impatience and greed."*
> —JIM ROHN

The most successful—and most content—people I know take joy in the journey toward their dreams. One of those people is Coach John Wooden. In *The Essential Wooden*, he writes about how much he enjoyed the process of working during his career:

> If I could go back and pick one single day in my life—in sports—to live over again, my choice might surprise you.
>
> It would not be that day in 1927 when our Martinsville High School basketball team won the Indiana state championship. Nor would it be any game I played as a member of the Purdue Boilermakers or coached at Indiana State Teachers College or UCLA.
>
> Here's the day I would pick if I could go back in time: I would like to conduct one more day of practice in the gym.

Each day of practice was, by far, the most fulfilling, exciting, and memorable thing I did as a coach—teaching those under my supervision how to achieve success as members of a team.

"The journey is better than the inn," Cervantes wrote. The struggle, the planning, the teaching and learning, the seeking (which, of course, is the journey) surpass all else for me, including records, titles, or national championships.

The awards and acknowledgment, the final score, all have their respective place, and I do not discount them. But, for me, Cervantes had it right: My joy was in the journey.

Perhaps you might examine the source of your own happiness —joy. Is it in your journey or only in the prize, the inn?[13]

Wooden accomplished more as a coach than almost any other in any sport. People dream of having just a fraction of his success. Yet his delight wasn't in his eight national championships. It wasn't in his perfect season. It was in the journey.

5. FULFILLED PEOPLE MAKE NEW DISCOVERIES WHILE
    LIVING IN THE GAP

If you keep moving forward toward your dream, and you keep your eyes open along the way, you will eventually find open doors that will lead to wonderful discoveries. Scientist Koichi Tanaka describes this phenomenon and how it can come about during the enjoyable pursuit of a dream. As he worked on trying to create an ion with lasers, he says, "I failed for weeks and months before I succeeded in making an ion. Why did I continue the experiment? Because I enjoyed it. It was fun for me to come to know something that I had never known before, and that fun enabled me to be persistent." That persistence helped him to win a Nobel Prize in chemistry.

You have the potential to make many wonderful discoveries in the pursuit of your dream. None will be greater than what you discover about yourself. I know that has been true for me. As you follow your dream, you will find that you can be more persistent than you thought. You can be more resourceful than you imagined. You can go places and do things that you never thought possible.

> *You have the potential to make many wonderful*
> *discoveries in the pursuit of your dream. None will be*
> *greater than what you discover about yourself.*

The pursuit of my dream has taken me out of my comfort zone, elevated my thinking, given me confidence, and confirmed my sense of purpose. My pursuit of the dream and my personal growth have become so intertwined that I now ask myself, *Did I make the dream, or did the dream make me?*

Author Thomas Merton wrote that we already have what we need. By that he meant that we don't need to chase things outside ourselves in order to find fulfillment. It's really a matter of attitude. We can choose to be content, to be satisfied with our lives—not by settling, but by discovering and by striving for our dreams. The greatest value of your dream won't be what you get from it; it will be who you become by pursuing it. In the end, it is not our dreams that we conquer. It is ourselves. You and I can discover ourselves if we are willing to look for fulfillment in the gap.

The human spirit is a miracle. Once it accepts a new idea or learns a new truth, it is forever changed. Once stretched, it takes on a new shape and never goes back to its original form. When we discover growth on the inside, we experience gains on the outside. And when that happens, we become fulfilled. No wonder children's book author Elizabeth Coatsworth said, "When I dream, I am ageless."

> *In the end, it is not our dreams that we conquer. It is ourselves.*

6. Fulfilled People Buy In to the Natural Law of Balance: Life Is Both Good and Bad

Optimists tend to think that all of life is good. Pessimists believe it's all bad. The reality is that neither is right. Life is both. Only people who accept *and* embrace that truth are able to find fulfillment. Why? Because people who accept it but don't embrace it become apathetic, meeting every difficulty with a shrug and a sigh. They may survive, but they will not be successful.

To reach a dream—and to be fulfilled in the process—one needs to be proactive, in bad times as well as good. One of the things I've observed about successful people over the years is that they do what is right no matter how they feel, and by doing right, they feel good. On the other hand, unsuccessful people wait to feel good before they do what is right. As a result, they neither do what's right nor feel good.

When you are traveling in the gap toward your dream, the majority of the time you will not feel like doing the right thing to enable your dream to come true. You'll need to do it anyway. That's what Nelson Mandela has done. He has done the right thing no matter how he feels about it. He says, "I have discovered the secret that after climbing a great hill, one finds many more hills to climb. I have taken a moment here to rest, to steal a view of the glorious vista that surrounds me, to look back on the distance I have come. But I can rest only for a moment, for with freedom come responsibilities, and I dare not linger, for my long walk is not yet ended."[14]

> *Successful people do what is right no matter how they feel, and by doing right, they feel good.*

If you can always do the right thing—despite how you feel, despite the circumstances, despite what others might say or do in response—you will be satisfied with yourself. And that, at the end of the day, will do a lot to determine whether you feel fulfilled.

LOVE THE JOURNEY

There's an old saying that if you love your job, you'll never work a day in your life. I don't think that's quite true. Most people work very hard even if they love their jobs. They must do things they don't like to do. They must give effort above and beyond what's comfortable. It's probably more accurate to say that if you're doing something you believe in, the hard work you do will bring you deep satisfaction. The work will be fulfilling.

Novelist Ursula K. Le Guin stated, "It is good to have an end to journey towards, but it is the journey that matters in the end." I've known many people who had destination disease. They think that arriving at a certain place in life will bring them happiness. What a shame. Because the reality is that many times, when we arrive where we hoped we would, we discover that it wasn't what we expected. If you become fixated on a destination—even a dream destination— you can miss all the great things that happen along the way. And you miss the joy of today. If you're convinced that someday is going to be your best day, you won't put enough into today—or get enough out of it.

If you're not doing something with your life, it doesn't matter how long it is. It's not enough to just survive. You need to really live. There's nothing extraordinary about simply going the distance from life to death. Going the distance—that was Rocky Balboa's goal in the original *Rocky* movie. He figured he didn't have a chance to win, so he made it his goal simply to stay in the fight, not embarrass himself too badly, not get knocked out. Prior to his shot at the big fight, he had no goals. He was merely existing, reacting to what others did around him. But something happened when he set that first goal, had that first dream. He made discoveries in the process of pursuing it. He discovered that there was more to him than he thought. He enjoyed the journey, and that led him to dream bigger dreams. And of course, in later movies, he went on to win the heavyweight championship of the world.

If you're not doing something with your life, it doesn't matter how long it is. It's not enough to just survive. You need to really live.

Rocky, of course, is a fictional character. But his journey reveals basic truths about what it means to find satisfaction in the pursuit of a dream. The process is everything. Who you *become* in the process makes a difference. And if you can find contentment in the journey toward your dream, if you can answer yes to the Fulfillment Question, then you can go to bed at the end of the day knowing that you lived that day well, no matter what tomorrow brings.

CAN YOU ANSWER YES TO
THE FULFILLMENT QUESTION:
DOES WORKING TOWARD MY DREAM
BRING SATISFACTION?

If you cannot answer yes to the Fulfillment Question, then you have the wrong dream, or you have the wrong attitude about it. If you hate what you must do in order to pursue your dream, then you are on the wrong path. Examine your motives. Try to discern why you have set your dream as your goal. Are there inconsistencies between who you are and what you're trying to accomplish? I don't mean to be repetitious, but you may need to revisit the Ownership Question one more time. Or perhaps your answer to the Passion Question hasn't been honest. Or maybe you are paying too high a price for your dream. If the pursuit of your dream causes you to violate your values, then you need to get another dream.

Maybe the problem is your attitude. Then examine how you approach living in the gap between the identification of your dream and its realization:

Are you too idealistic? Stop expecting everything to be perfect. Accept the way your dream is unfolding instead of holding out for perfection. Remember that life is both good and bad.

Is the size of the gap discouraging you? If your dreams are huge, then so is the gap. Change your expectations concerning how long it will take you to achieve your dream. Ninety percent of all disappointment stems from unrealistic expectations.

Have you stopped daily dreaming? When some people start pursuing their dream, they think it means they have to be all business. Not so. Let yourself dream a little bit every day. Explore possibilities.

Embrace options. Be creative. Continuing to dream actually helps you move forward.

Are you appreciating the small steps forward? One way to feel fulfilled in the journey is to celebrate your successes. Recognize when you pass milestones. Giving yourself credit for progress will encourage you to keep working and moving forward.

Have you made personal discovery and growth your goal? The surest way to reach a big dream is to enlarge yourself. The bigger the dream, the bigger the person must be to achieve it. What can you learn about yourself in your current situation? How can you grow? Never forget that the greatest reward of pursuing a dream is who you become as a result.

CHAPTER 10

The Significance Question
Does My Dream Benefit Others?

If a man for whatever reason has the opportunity to lead
an extraordinary life, he has no right to keep it to himself.

–JACQUES-YVES COUSTEAU

You must ask yourself one final question if you truly want to put your dream to the test, to measure whether it is a dream worth dedicating your life to. It is not a complicated question. In fact, you will find that this is the shortest chapter in this book. However, this final question has the most far-reaching impact. It is the Significance Question: Does my dream benefit others?

WHO WILL YOUR DREAM BENEFIT?

On a bookshelf in my office is a group of books that I highly prize. They aren't the oldest books I own. Nor are they the most valuable. Something of a collector, I do own a few of value: my collection of the novels of Horatio Alger and some original volumes written by seventeenth-century church leader John Wesley. No, the books on this particular shelf have no monetary value at all, but they have great personal value. They are the books that have had the greatest impact on my life. Each represents a different phase of my life and was instrumental in helping me move forward in life's journey. I often find myself returning to this small section of books, pulling one down, reading the notes I wrote in the margins or on the flyleaf, and giving thanks for the way the author's thoughts influenced and assisted my development as a person.

As I worked on *Put Your Dream to the Test,* the book I pulled off the shelf was *Halftime* by Bob Buford. The subtitle captures what the book is really about. It reads, "Changing Your Game Plan from Success to Significance." It is a book that greatly influenced me when I was in my midforties.

"The first half of life," writes Buford, "has to do with getting and gaining, learning and earning. The second half is more risky because it has to do with living beyond the immediate."[1] Those words definitely challenged me. They made me think about living beyond myself and striving to be bigger than my natural selfishness.

> *"The first half of life has to do with getting and gaining, learning and earning. The second half is more risky because it has to do with living beyond the immediate."*
> —BOB BUFORD

The great men and women of history were not great because of what they earned and owned. They were great because they gave themselves to people and causes that lived beyond them. Their dream was to do something that benefited others. A rare minority of people are able to hold closely to their dream to make a difference and are willing to give up everything to make that dream come true. Of people like that, it will never be said that when they died, it was as though they never lived. Their dream lives on after them because they lived for others. They were able to answer yes to the Significance Question: Does my dream benefit others?

AMAZING TALENT

One of the most remarkable stories I've ever read about someone who transitioned from incredibly selfish ambitions to exceptionally unselfish dreams is William Wilberforce, a name that was recently unknown to many until the movie *Amazing Grace* was released. The dream that captivated Wilberforce was the abolition of slavery, and he ended up dedicating his life to it.

Wilberforce was born in England in 1759, when the British slave trade was in full swing and much of Britain's economy depended on it. His father died when he was a boy, and he spent part of his youth with a religious aunt and uncle. It was at their house when he was probably ten or eleven years old that he first learned about slavery. There he met John Newton, a former slave ship captain who had repented of his old life and had become an Anglican priest. However, there wasn't much evidence that the meeting made a lasting impression on Wilberforce until several years later.

Wilberforce grew up a child of privilege and wealth. He attended Cambridge but didn't distinguish himself academically. He was known more for his charm, his wit, and his ability to entertain his friends. While others studied, he had parties and traded quips with other students. You could say that he made the least of his time—something he regretted later in life.

A person of immense natural talent, at age twenty, Wilberforce got it into his head to run for election to the House of Commons. In those days, success in politics came as the result of two things: rhetorical skill and wealth. Wilberforce had both in abundance. In a matter of months, he spent £9,000, a huge sum, to advance his candidacy. Two weeks after his twenty-first birthday, he was elected to Parliament, having won the same number of votes as the combined total of his two opponents.

Wilberforce was immediately well received and popular in London's political circles. He was quickly admitted to five exclusive clubs frequented by members of Parliament, where they dined and gambled. Though small in stature, he made a big impression. His interpersonal skills were unsurpassed. He had an excellent singing voice, which he was known to use in entertaining his friends. Some called him "the wittiest man in all of England."[2] And he was a first-rate orator whose voice people found mesmerizing. By the time he had been in Parliament a few years, few could match his rhetorical skills. Biographer Eric Metaxas observes that at age twenty-four, "He seemed unstoppable. With his extraordinary eloquence, brilliance, and charm—and with the prime minister [William Pitt] as his dearest friend—there seemed no end in sight to where he might rise."[3]

But to what would he rise? Beyond making it to Parliament and succeeding there—which might have been a difficult goal to achieve for nearly anyone else—he had no dreams. He was ambitious and he was talented, but he was also directionless. Years later Wilberforce remarked, "The first years I was in Parliament I did nothing—nothing to any purpose. My own distinction was my darling object."[4] He was in genuine danger of wasting his life.

AMAZING DREAM

All that began to change in 1784 when Wilberforce started to explore the religious faith of his youth. And in the process, he experienced what he described as the "Great Change." It marked him permanently. Two years later, he was a different person, and the changes gave birth to dreams bigger than his own petty wants. He desired to help the poor people in England and to address the many social problems that plagued the nation: epidemic alcoholism, child prostitution, lack of education for the poor, crime, brutal public executions, and animal cruelty. He immediately threw himself into this work. But another important work became his dream a few years later: the abolition of slavery.

The practice of slavery is said to be as old as humanity, and the world's most ancient literary and legal manuscripts tend to support this view. However, during the sixteenth and seventeenth centuries, a particularly brutal version was being practiced in the Western Hemisphere, and England was at the center of it. English slave ships departed from Britain's shores carrying goods to Africa. Once there, they unloaded those goods for sale and sailed up and down the coast, buying people from African slave traders who made their living kidnapping men, women, and children to be sold into slavery. Once the holds of their ships were crammed full of chained and shackled people, the captains embarked on the long and brutally painful voyage across the Atlantic Ocean to the West Indies where the African slaves were sold. Most were literally worked to death in just a few years on the sugar plantations there. Others were sold in the American colonies that became the United States.

Most people in England in the 1780s were completely unaware of this continually occurring chain of events. As Wilberforce became well acquainted with what was happening, he determined to dedicate himself to ending the British slave trade. He saw it as his duty and as a major part of his purpose for living. Wilberforce remarked, "Strange that the most generous men and religious, do not see that their duties increase with their fortune, and that they will be punished for spending it [on themselves]."[5]

Beginning in 1787, Wilberforce initiated his campaign. He believed that if the members of Parliament became aware of the atrocities of slavery, they would vote for its abolition at once. He and other proponents of abolition gathered overwhelming evidence of the slave trade's brutality in every stage and presented it to Parliament. In his first speech on the subject, Wilberforce said:

> So much misery condensed in so little room is more than the human imagination has ever before conceived. . . . So enormous, so dreadful, so irremediable did its wickedness appear, that my own mind was completely made up for the abolition. A trade founded in iniquity, and carried on as this was, must be abolished, let the price be what it might—let the consequences be what they would, I from this time determined that I would never rest till I had [secured] its abolition.[6]

Despite Wilberforce's eloquence and the overwhelming evidence presented against slavery, he could not get the votes needed to abolish it.

The next year, Wilberforce and his friends made everyone in the nation aware of slavery's ills. Poets published verse about it. An engraving of how men, women, and children were stacked in the hold of a slave ship was posted in shop windows and hung on tavern walls throughout England. Songs against slavery were sung. Essays were published. Josiah Wedgwood created a cameo with the image of a chained slave containing the caption, "Am I not a man and a brother?" Public sentiment against slavery was strong, but still they could not get the votes needed to end it.

For twenty years, Wilberforce fought against slavery. From 1787 to 1807, bills to abolish the slave trade were presented to Parliament eleven times and defeated every time. Wilberforce might have given up if it weren't for the encouragement of others who knew he was trying to do the right thing. One of them was preacher John Wesley. At age eighty-seven, Wesley wrote his last letter before his death and sent it to Wilberforce. It said:

Dear Sir:

Unless the divine power has raised you up to be as *Athanasius contra mundum* [one man against the whole world], I see not how you can go through your glorious enterprise in opposing that execrable villainy which is the scandal of religion, of England, and of human nature. Unless God has raised you up for this very thing, you will be worn out by the opposition of men and devils. But if God be for you, who can be against you? Are all of them together stronger than God? O be not weary of well doing! Go on, in the name of God and in the power of his might, till even American slavery (the vilest that ever saw the sun) shall vanish away before it.

Reading this morning a tract wrote by a poor African, I was particularly struck by that circumstance that a man who has a black skin, being wronged or outraged by a white man, can have no redress; it being a "law" in our colonies that the oath of a black against a white goes for nothing. What villainy is this?

That he who has guided you from youth up may continue to strengthen you in this and all things, is the prayer of, dear sir,

Your affectionate servant,

John Wesley[7]

Wilberforce persevered because he knew what was at stake: the lives of millions of people. Finally, on February 23, 1807, after having already been presented to and passed by the House of Lords, the Slave Trade Act outlawing traffic in slaves was passed in the House of Commons by a vote of 283 to 16. The first stage of Wilberforce's dream had come to pass. And though it took another twenty-six years, and by then Wilberforce had passed the baton to someone else in Parliament, the second phase of his dream was realized in 1833 when the House of Commons voted to outlaw the practice of slavery in the British Empire. Three days later Wilberforce died.

AMAZING IMPACT

It's difficult to gauge the impact that the realization of Wilberforce's dream has had on the world. It's obvious that it helped innumerable people who otherwise would have been sold into slavery. However, writer Eric Metaxas argues that the impact of the abolition of the slave trade has even greater implications. He writes that as soon as Wilberforce had succeeded,

> We had suddenly entered a world in which we would never again ask whether it was our responsibility as a society to help the poor and suffering. We would only quibble about how. . . . Once this idea was loosed upon the world, the world changed. Slavery and the slave trade would soon be largely abolished, but many lesser social evils would be abolished too. For the first time in history, groups sprang up for every possible social cause.[8]

That's why Metaxas calls Wilberforce "the greatest social reformer in the history of the world." Metaxas goes on to say, "The world he was born into in 1759 and the world he departed in 1833 were as different as lead and gold. Wilberforce presided over a social earthquake that rearranged the continents and whose magnitude we are only now beginning to fully appreciate."[9]

A QUESTION ANSWERED IN PHASES

I believe it can be difficult to answer the Significance Question definitively in one's younger years. In the early phases of life, we are often occupied with discovering our talents, exploring our possibilities, and searching for our purpose. That's good. But the older we get, the healthier it is for us to focus outward, to imagine dreams that will benefit others, not just ourselves. For most people, it is a process. And here's good news: it's never too late to help others, and most people make their most significant contributions not when they're young, but when they're older.

The ability to answer yes to the Significance Question—Does my dream benefit others?—has come in stages for me. That might be the same for you. Take a look at how it has unfolded in my life, represented by these three statements:

1. I Want to Do Something Significant for Myself

When you read that statement, I bet you think it is pretty selfish, don't you? Your first reaction may be to distance yourself from it, especially in light of the subject of this chapter. I hope you don't do that, and here's why: this sentiment is not necessarily just self-serving.

For example, the last time you were on a plane, you probably heard the flight attendants give instructions about what to do in an emergency. If the plane loses cabin pressure and passengers need to use oxygen masks, what are they supposed to do first? Put on their own mask and *then* help others. Why is that? Because it is impossible to help others if you haven't taken care of yourself.

I believe the accomplishment of a significant dream comes only when a person has something to offer. That means creating a personal foundation from which he can work and serve. In the case of William Wilberforce, his launching point was holding a seat in Parliament. He had to have a place in government to make a difference. For me, it was building a church. I had to learn leadership and become a better communicator before I could add value to people. For you, it may mean building a career or getting an education or earning money that can be used to serve others. If you haven't done anything significant to help yourself, how will you be able to help others?

> *The accomplishment of a significant dream comes only when a person has something to offer.*

When I speak to an audience of leaders, I frequently ask them two important questions: (1) "What are you doing to invest in yourself?" and (2) "What are you doing to invest in others?" Unless people invest in themselves, they have a very difficult time trying to invest in others. You cannot give to others what you yourself do not have.

2. I Want to Do Something Significant for Others

Often when we start out in life, we are a lot like William Wilberforce. We are ambitious. Our goal is to get ahead. We want to achieve things for our own benefit. Soichiro Honda, founder of Honda motorcycles, said that his early vision wasn't about building a big company or accomplishing any other lofty goals. He admitted, "I happened on the idea of fitting an engine to a bicycle simply because I did not want to ride crowded trains and buses." But there comes a time in the lives of all successful people when they have to make a choice. Are they going to climb the mountain of success for themselves, or are they going to climb it so that they can reach down, lift others up, and help climb?

Let's face it: success can cause people to be selfish. If you make the most of your natural talent and work hard, you can become a schemer who asks, "What can I get from others?" Would it not be better to become a dreamer who asks, "What can I give to others?"

> *What are you doing to invest in yourself, and*
> *what are you doing to invest in others?*

If you answer yes to the Significance Question and your dream will benefit others, then you are on the right track. That doesn't mean you need to save the whole world. You should start small and give it your best.

Recently I read a book titled *Mother Teresa—Come Be My Light: The Private Writings of the Saint of Calcutta*. It contains many of the heartfelt letters that Mother Teresa wrote to her superiors containing her private thoughts about her life and calling to serve people. In one letter, she wrote about the potential success of the Missionaries of Charity organization that she founded:

> I don't know what the success will be—but if the Missionaries of Charity have brought joy to one unhappy home—made one innocent child from the street keep pure for Jesus—one dying person die in peace with God—don't you think, Your Grace, it would be worth while offering everything—for just that one—because that one would bring great joy to the Heart of Jesus.[10]

Few people would dispute the impact that Mother Teresa made in her lifetime. She inspired millions of people, sat with presidents and kings, and modeled servanthood to the world. Yet, as you can see, her dream of helping others started small, with the goal of affecting one unhappy home, one innocent child, or one dying person. She once said, "A day lived without doing something good for others is a day not worth living."

> "A day lived without doing something good
> for others is a day not worth living."
> —MOTHER TERESA

Nelson Mandela, another person whose dream benefited many other people, also grew into his dream. At first, he was motivated by dreams of freedom for himself. But before long, his dream expanded to include others. He stated:

I slowly saw that not only was I not free, but my brothers and sisters were not free. I saw that it was not just my freedom that was curtailed, but the freedom of everyone who looked like I did. That is when I joined the African [National] Congress, and that is when the hunger for my own freedom became the greater hunger for the freedom of my people. It was this desire for the freedom of my people to live their lives with dignity and self-respect that animated my life, that transformed a frightened young man into a bold one, that drove a law-abiding attorney to become a criminal, that turned a family-loving man into a man without a home, that forced a life-loving man to live like a monk.[11]

When Mandela found himself at the crossroads of life—with

one path leading to personal gain and the other to serving his people—he chose the more difficult higher road of helping others. And look at the impact he has made.

> *"I never perfected an invention without thinking in terms of how it would benefit others."*
> —Thomas Edison

Have you yet been confronted with that decision? It doesn't mean abandoning your dream. It means expanding it! Thomas Edison said, "I never perfected an invention without thinking in terms of how it would benefit others." He didn't stop being an inventor so that he could help others. William Wilberforce didn't quit Parliament to help others, though he considered it at one point. No, each used what he had already accomplished for himself, and he put it to good use for others. They adopted an attitude of service toward their fellow human beings.

Too often when we're starting out, we dream of doing earth-changing things, and the thought of tackling them intimidates us. That is yet another reason to start small. If you are in the second phase of growth in answering the Significance Question, don't try to help everyone. Just try to help someone! Do that, and in time you may find yourself living what Saint Francis of Assisi described when he said, "Start doing what is necessary; then do what is possible; and suddenly, you are doing the impossible." But even if you never get to do big things, you will find great contentment in doing right things. No act of kindness is too small to be worth doing.

3. I Want to Do Something Significant with Others

Retired television newsman Tom Brokaw observed, "It's easy to make a buck. It's a lot tougher to make a difference." One reason is that making a real difference requires teamwork. Mother Teresa did not make a difference on her own. Neither did Nelson Mandela or William Wilberforce. Their dreams were large, and as a result, they required the participation of many others to bring them to pass.

People who want to achieve a significant dream *with others* must be able to help other people embrace that same dream. And when they do, what a wonderful gift it is for all of them. If you and I can share a dream with others, it expands both their possibilities and our own.

At age sixty-one as I look back on my dream journey, it makes me smile. Little did I realize, when I started with a desire to add significance to others, that it would add significance to me! Now I understand. We *should not* receive anything without giving, and we *cannot* give anything without receiving in return. Our lives are to be rivers, not reservoirs. Adding value to others is the surest way to add value to our own lives.

> *We* should not *receive anything without giving, and* we cannot *give anything without receiving in return.*

Pursing a dream *with* others has meant practicing together, sacrificing together, working together, planning together, communicating together, winning together, and celebrating together! What a wonderful thing. That is what community is all about. It's a group whose members make an intentional transition from "the community for myself" to "myself for the community." To give oneself to a cause that adds value to others and to join people to accomplish that aim is the ultimate high in living the dream.

Years ago, author and speaker Florence Littauer taught a lesson that impressed this truth upon me. She offered the following sequence of steps for developing a dream that positively answers the Significance Question:

Dare to dream—To dream means taking a risk, stepping out of your comfortable surroundings and situation.

Prepare the dream—The set-up determines the success. All is well that begins well. Preparation gives your dream a chance.

Wear the dream—Put it on. Your dream is not an addendum to your life; it is your life.

Repair the dream—Continual maintenance is needed to keep the dream going. Dreams need constant tender loving care.

Share the dream—Pass it on to others. Give them ownership and then accomplish the dream together.

A dream isn't worthy of a person's life if it doesn't benefit others. And it isn't fulfilling unless it is achieved with others. That is why we're here: to help other people. As Woodrow Wilson stated, "You are not here merely to make a living. You are here in order to enable the world to live more amply, with greater vision, with a finer spirit of hope and achievement. You are here to enrich the world, and you impoverish yourself if you forget the errand."

HOW DO YOU ANSWER
THE SIGNIFICANCE QUESTION?

There's an old Middle Eastern blessing that says, "When you were born, you cried, and the world rejoiced. May you live your life so that when you die, the world will cry, and you will rejoice." Whether or not that blessing becomes true in our lives depends in large part on how we answer the Significance Question.

At the beginning of this chapter, I mentioned *Halftime*. In it Bob Buford asks, "As you work to carry out your dream, what difference will it make fifty or a hundred or five hundred years from now?"[12] The dreams of the people I mention in this chapter are still making an impact. It's been more than 175 years since Wilberforce died, and the impact of his dream is still being felt. If your dream does not benefit others, if it helps only you, then it won't matter even five minutes after you're gone.

What have you set your dream sights on? Are you struggling for survival? Are you seeking success? Or are you striving for significance? The choice is really yours! What kind of dream will you give your life to? You've probably heard the expression, "What a difference a day makes." We all know that to be true. A birth, a death, a marriage, an opportunity, a tragedy—each can change a life in just one day. But it can also be said, "What a difference a dream makes." Someone with a significant dream can become the catalyst for change in our world. You can answer yes to the Significance Question, and neither you nor others will ever be the same. What a wonderful dream.

CAN YOU ANSWER YES TO
THE SIGNIFICANCE QUESTION:
DOES MY DREAM BENEFIT OTHERS?

At what stage of life do you currently find yourself?

Are you simply surviving? If so, it's time to take steps toward success. You cannot give what you do not have. Create a foundation and platform for giving to others by doing something significant for yourself. If you are not already pursuing your dream, get moving!

Are you already achieving success? If you are, perhaps you are nearing the crossroads where you must decide whether you will live for yourself or for others. How can you expand your dream to include others and help them to benefit from what you have already achieved?

Are you striving for significance? If so, then it's time to take your contribution to the next level. One is too small a number to achieve greatness. Dream bigger and include others in your dream. Lead others to join you in the process. It will enlarge you, enlarge them, and benefit more people in a much more significant way. What do you feel called or destined to do? Who are you most qualified to serve? How can you best add value to others in the time you have in this life?

Looking Back . . . Looking Forward

In 1969, I began to dream about making a difference in the lives of people. After ten years of following that vision, I thought about whether I was succeeding. To my surprise, the first thing I discovered was that my dream to help others had helped me!

Now looking back, I can see that has always been the case for me. Here's how:

- *My dream has helped me to focus.* Every time I was tempted to stray away from my purpose, my dream kept me headed in the right direction.
- *My dream has helped me to stretch.* Often, I wanted to stay in my comfort zone, but my dream always propelled me out of it and challenged me to keep growing.
- *My dream has helped me to sacrifice.* When the prize for success got high, my dream encouraged me to pay it, reminding me that there are no shortcuts to success.
- *My dream has helped me to persevere.* When I thought about my dream, quitting was not an option. No one ever arrived at his

dream destination by stopping. Dreams don't come to us; we must go to them.

⊛ *My dream has helped me to attract winners.* The size of my dream determined the size of the people who were attracted to it. Small dreams attract small people. Big dreams attract big people.

⊛ *My dream has helped me to depend on God and others.* My dream was too big for me. I needed God and others to help me. They did, and everyone won!

Your dream can do the same for you—but only if you put your dream to the test and are able to answer yes to the questions in this book.

As you've observed, in each chapter I've told the story of someone whose journey highlighted the particular question I was teaching. I hope you found those stories helpful. However, the truth is that I could have used the example of any of those people to illustrate one of the other chapters of the book. Why do I say that? Because if asked, all of them would have answered yes to all ten questions in the book. Take another look at the questions:

1. The Ownership Question: Is my dream really my dream?

2. The Clarity Question: Do I clearly see my dream?

3. The Reality Question: Am I depending on factors within my control to achieve my dream?

4. The Passion Question: Does my dream compel me to follow it?

5. The Pathway Question: Do I have a strategy to reach my dream?

6.   The People Question: Have I included the people I need to realize my dream?

7.   The Cost Question: Am I willing to pay the price for my dream?

8.   The Tenacity Question: Am I moving closer to my dream?

9.   The Fulfillment Question: Does working toward my dream bring satisfaction?

10.   The Significance Question: Does my dream benefit others?

Every person owned his or her dream. Every one of them saw it clearly. They all depended on their own skills, talent, hard work, and other factors within their control to go after their dream. All of them were filled with a passion that compelled them to follow their dream. Each one had a strategy to achieve it. They were assisted by others, paid a price to move forward, were tenacious in their efforts, and found fulfillment in working to see their dream become reality. And all of them made efforts to benefit others, not just themselves, along the way.

I mention that because I want to remind you that if you desire to live your dream, you cannot afford to answer yes to just one or two or a few of these questions. The more times you can answer yes, the greater the odds that you will achieve your dream. And that's a good thing, because when you achieve your dream, the world becomes a better place.

NOTES

Introduction

1. Gary Hamel and C. K. Prahalad, *Competing for the Future* (Cambridge, MA: Harvard Business School Press, 1996), 55–56.
2. Mark Twain, *Following the Equator* (Hartford, CT: The American Publishing Company, 1897).
3. Quote by Bruce Lockerbie. Used with permission.
4. Kenneth Hildebrand, *Achieving Real Happiness* (New York: Harper & Brothers, 1955).
5. Karen Lynn Eve Greno-Malsch, "Children's Use of Interpersonal Negotiation Strategies as a Function of Their Level of Self-worth" (PhD diss., University of Wisconsin, Milwaukee, 1998).
6. Max Lucado, *The Applause of Heaven* (Nashville: Word Publishing, a division of Thomas Nelson, 1999), 175.
7. Howard Schultz, *Pour Your Heart Into It: How Starbucks Built a Company One Cup at a Time* (New York: Hyperion Books, 1999).

Chapter 1

1. Cecil G. Osborne, *The Art of Understanding Yourself* (Grand Rapids, MI: Zondervan, 1987).
2. Arnold Schwarzenegger and Douglas Kent Hall, *Arnold: The Education of a Bodybuilder* (New York: Simon and Schuster Paperbacks, 1977), 14.
3. Laurence Leamer, *Fantastic: The Life of Arnold Schwarzenegger* (New York: St. Martin's, 2005), 25.
4. Schwarzenegger and Hall, *Arnold*, 33.
5. Ibid., 16–17.
6. Ibid., 81–82.
7. Leamer, *Fantastic,* 66.

8. Arnold Schwarzenegger," Box Office Mojo, http://www.boxofficemojo.com/people/chart/?id=arnoldschwarzenegger.htm (accessed January 4, 2008).

9. Mark Matthews, "Gov. Schwarzenegger's Tax Returns Released," April 15, 2006, http://abclocal.go.com/kgo/story?section=politics&id=4085877 (accessed January 4, 2008).

10. Schwarzenegger and Hall, *Arnold*, 31.

11. Joseph Brodsky, The Nobel Prize in Literature 1987, Nobel Lecture 8 December 1987. http://nobelprize.org/nobel_prizes/literature/laureates/1987/brodsky-lecture-e.html (accessed 10 Octoboer 2008)

12. Rodney Dangerfield, *It's Not Easy Bein' Me* (New York: HarperCollins, 2004), p. xi.

13. The quote that Dr. Larabee has Akeelah read from a plaque on his wall is an excerpt from *A Return To Love: Reflections on the Principles of a Course in Miracles* by Marianne Williamson (New York: HarperCollins, 1996).

14. *Akeelah and The Bee* written and directed by Doug Atchison. © 2006 Spelling Bee Productions, Inc./ Lions Gate Films.

15. Don Freeman, "Irving Berlin Brought Us Blue Skies for 8 Decades," *The San Diego Union* 22 May 2004.

16. Po Bronson, *What Should I Do with My Life* (New York: Ballantine Books, a division of Random House, 2005).

17. Commencement Remarks MIT Graduation by Carelton "Carly" Fiorina, 2 June 2000.

18. *Webster's New World Dictionary of American English, Third College Edition* (Cleveland: Webster's New World, 1991).

19. Anna Quindlen's Commencement Speech, Mount Holyoke College, 23 May 1999. www.mtholyoke.edu/offices/comm/oped/Quindlen.shtml (accessed 14 August 2008.

20. Robert Kriegel and Louis Patler, *If IT Ain't Broke... Break It!* (New York: Warner Books, 1992).

Chapter 2

1. Joseph McBride, *Steven Spielberg: A Biography* (Cambridge MA: Da Capo Press, a division of Perseus, 1999), 13.

2. *Mental Floss*, March-April 2007, 45.

3 "Diamond Jewelry: Famous Diamonds: The Star of South Africa," http://www.adiamondisforever.com/jewelry/famous_starsa.html (accessed January 24, 2008).

4. "De Beers History," http://www.debeersgroup.com/debeersweb/ About+De+Beers/De+Beers+History/ (accessed January 24, 2008).

Chapter 3

1. John Wooden and Steve Jamison, *The Essential Wooden* (Columbus, OH: McGraw-Hill, 2006), 24.
2. Catherine Ahles, "The Dynamics of Discovery: Creating Your Own Opportunities," Delivered to Phi Theta Kappa, Macomb Community College, Center Campus, Warren, Michigan, December 11, 1992. http:// scilib.univ.kiev.ua/doc.php?7198252 (accessed 15 October 2008).
3. Jack Canfield and Gay Hendricks with Carol Kline, *You've Got to Read This Book!,* Kindle Edition (New York: HarperCollins e-books, 2006), 1642–52.
4. "Timeline," http://www.drfarrahgray.com/timeline.html (accessed January 31, 2008).
5. "Michael Jordan: The Stats," http://www.infoplease.com/ipsa/A0779388. html (accessed February 25, 2008).
6. Robert Ringer, *Million Dollar Habits* (New York: Fawcett, 1990).

Chapter 4

1. William Arthur Ward, "Believe While Others Are Doubting." Used by permission. All rights reserved.
2. Richard Edler, *If I Knew Then What I Know Now CEOs and Other Smart Executives Share Wisdom They Wish They'd Been Told 25 Years Ago.*(New York: G.P. Putnam's Sons, 1996).
3. Logan Pearsall Smith, *Afterthoughts* (London: Constable, 1931).
4. Michael John Simmons, *Taylor Guitars: 30 Years of a New American Classic* (Bergkirchen, Germany: PPV Medien, 2003), 13.
5. Ibid., 33.
6. Ibid., 36.
7. Ibid., 56.
8. Ibid., 58.
9. Ibid., 138.
10. Ibid., 154.
11. Ibid., 191.
12. Ibid., 21.

13. James Kouzes and Barry Posner, *The Leadership Challenge* (Hoboken, NJ: Jossey-Bass, a division of Wiley & Sons, 2002).
14. Simmons, 33.

Chapter 5

1. "Lab Overview," Media Lab, http://www.media.mit.edu/?page_id=13 (accessed February 12, 2008).
2. "About Nicholas Negroponte, the Author of Being Digital," http://archives.obs-us.com/obs/english/books/nn/nnbio.htm (accessed February 12, 2008).
3. "Mission: Provide Children Around the World with New Opportunities to Explore," http://www.laptop.org/en/vision/mission/index.shtml (accessed February 7, 2008).
4. Peter Apps, "World's Poorest Don't Want '$100 Laptop'—Intel," http://web.archive.org/web/20051212065117/http://www.alertnet.org/thenews/newsdesk/SP263515.htm, December 9, 2005 (accessed February 11, 2008).
5. "Nicholas Negroponte: The Vision Behind One Laptop Per Child," speech delivered at TED, February 2006, http://www.ted.com/index.php/talks/view/id/41 (accessed February 12, 2008).
6. Wade Roush, "Nicholas Negroponte: The Interview," *Xconomy*, January 28, 2008, http://www.xconomy.com/2008/01/28/nicholas-negroponte-the-interview/ (accessed February 7, 2008.
7. Robert Buderi, "The Little Laptop That Could . . . One Way or Another," Xconomy, November 26, 2007, http://www.xconomy.com/2007/11/26/the-little-laptop-that-couldone-way-or-another/2/ (accessed February 11, 2008).
8. Hiawatha Bray, "One Laptop Per Child Orders Surge," *Boston Globe,* December 1, 2007, http://www.boston.com/business/globe/articles/2007/12/01/one_laptop_per_child_orders_surge/ (accessed February 13, 2008).
9. Obtained from ThinkTQ.com; more recent statistical findings posted at http://www.thinktq.com/training/articles/tqs_article.cfm?id=1364A81D073DBABF7C59DCFA476B864B indicate that current percentages are even lower than cited as of February 14, 2008.
10. Interview with George Lucas," Academy of Achievement, 19 June 1999. www.achievement.org/autodoc/page/luc0int-1 (accessed 15 August 2008).
11. Commencement Address by Christopher Matthews, May 16, 2004. www.hws.edu/news/transcripts/matthewscomm2004.aspx (accessed 15 August 2008).
12. Peter F. Drucker, *Management: Tasks, Responsibilities, Practices* (Piscataway, NJ: Transaction Publishers, 2008), 123–25.

13. Sam Walton and John Huey, *Made in America: My Story* (New York: Doubleday, 1992), 90.
14. Proverbs 27:12 (The Living Bible).
15. Wesley K. Clark, *Waging Modern War* (New York: PublicAffairs, a division of Perseus, 2001).

Chapter 6

1. Stephen R Covey, Roger Merrill, and Rebecca Merrill, *First Things First* (New York: Simon & Schuster, 1994).
2. Roger B. Stein, *John Ruskin and Aesthetic Thought in America, 1840-1900* (Cambridge, MA: 1967).
3. Studs Terkel, *Working* (New York: Simon & Schuster, 1974), xxiv.
4. John Wooden, Steve Jamison, *The Essential Wooden: A Lifetime of Lessons on Leaders and Leadership* (Columbus, OH: McGraw-Hill Professional, 2007), 143.
5. The "This was their finest hour" speech was first delivered by Sir Winston Churchill to the House of Commons of the Parliament of the United Kingdom on 18 June 1940.

Chapter 7

1. Kevin Myers, 12Stone™ Church. Used by permission. All rights reserved.
2. Ibid.
3. "The Importance of Starting Early," Investment Company Institute, http://www.ici.org/i4s/bro_i4s_early.html (accessed March 7, 2008). Example assumes 7 percent return per year and ignores the effects of taxes and inflation.
4. Max Lucado, *He Still Moves Stones* (Nashville: W Publishing Group, 1999), 158.
5. *Houston Chronicle*, May 3, 1996, 2D.
6. Jack Canfield, *The Success Principles:How to Get from Where You Are to Where You Want to Be* (New York: Collins Living, a division of HarperCollins, 2004).
7. Commencement Address by David Mamet, University of Vermont, May 2004. www.uvm.edu/~cmncmnt/commencement2004/?Page=mamet_commencementspeech04.html (accessed August 21, 2008).
8. Michael Ignatieff, Whitman Commencement Address 2004: "Living Fearlessly in a Fearful World." www.whitman.edu/content/news/LivingFearlesslyinaFearfulWorld (accessed 21 August 2008).

9. William Arthur Ward, "I Will Do More." Used by permission. All rights reserved.

10. "About Terry Fox," Terry Fox Run, http://www.terryfoxrun.org/english/about%20terry%20fox/default.asp?s=1 (accessed March 11, 2008).

11. "Top Ten Greatest Canadians: Terry Fox," the Greatest Canadian, http://www.cbc.ca/greatest/top_ten/nominee/fox-terry.html (accessed March 11, 2008).

12. Ibid.

13. Ibid.

14. "About Terry Fox," Terry Fox Run.

Chapter 8

1. Elizabeth Keckley, *Behind the Scenes: Or, Thirty Years a Slave, and Four Years in the White House* (New York: Penguin, 2005), 11–12.

2. Jennifer Fleischner, *Mrs. Lincoln and Mrs. Keckly: The Remarkable Story of the Friendship Between a First Lady and a Former Slave* (New York: Broadway, 2004), 124.

3. Ibid.

4. Keckley, *Behind the Scenes,* 20.

5. Ibid.

6. Ibid., 21.

7. Ibid., 24.

8. Ibid., 34.

9. Ibid., 83.

10. Fleischner, *Lincoln and Keckly,* 294.

11. Ibid., 297.

12. Jennifer Minar, "Oprah Pick Author Tawni O'Dell on Writing & the Importance of Perseverence," *Writer's Break*, 2003. www.writersbreak.com/interview_tawniodell.htm (accessed 21 August 2008).

13. Jack Canfield with Janet Switzer, *The Success Principles: How to Get from Where You Are to Where You Want to Be* (Collins Living, 2006), 104–105.

14. Jonas Salk Interview, "The Calling to Find a Cure," *Academy of Achievement,* 16 May 1991. www.achievement.org/autodoc/page/sal0int-1 (accessed 21 August 2008).

15. George Sweeting, *Great Quotes and Illustrations* (Waco: Word, 1985).

16. Canfield, *The Success Principles,* 178–179.

17. "The History of Chicken Soup for the Soul," http://www.chickensoup.com/cs.asp?cid=about (accessed March 17, 2008).

Chapter 9

1. Henry David Thoreau, *Walden, or Life in the Woods* (New York: Houghton Mifflin, 1949), xi.

2. Seth Godin, *The Dip*, Kindle Edition (New York: Penguin, 2007), 787–91.

3. "Forbes' List of the World's Richest Billionaires," March 8, 2007, http://www.usatoday.com/money/2007-03-08-forbes-billionaire-list_N.htm (accessed March 18, 2008).

4. Patrick James, "GOOD Q&A: Jacqueline Novogratz," November 27, 2007, http://www.goodmagazine.com/blog/acumen (accessed March 17, 2008).

5. Ibid.

6. Anne Field, "Investor in the World's Poor," Stanford Graduate School of Business, May 2007, http://www.gsb.stanford.edu/news/bmag/sbsm0705/feature_novogratz.html (accessed March 17, 2008).

7. Jacqueline Novogratz, "Tackling Poverty with 'Patient Capital,'" June 2007, http://www.ted.com/talks/view/id/157 (accessed March 18, 2008).

8. *The Next Garde,* video, http://www.sundancechannel.com/nextgarde/ (accessed March 18, 2008).

9. "About Us," Acumen Fund, http://www.acumenfund.org/about-us.html (accessed March 17, 2008).

10. "Acumen Fund Honored with Social Capitalist Award by Fast Company & Monitor Group," PR Web Press Release Newswire, http://www.prweb.com/releases/2007/12/prweb573845.htm (accessed March 17, 2008).

11. *The Next Garde.*

12. Dan Sullivan, "The Gap," audio message. (The strategic coach, inc., 2000)

13. John Steinbeck, *Journal of a Novel: The* East of Eden *Letters* (London: Penguin, 2001), 74–75.

14. John Wooden and Steve Jamison, *The Essential Wooden: A Lifetime of Lessons on Leaders and Leadership* (New York: McGraw-Hill, 2007), 184–85.

15. Nelson Mandela, *The Long Walk to Freedom* (New York: Holt Rinehart & Winston, 2000).

Chapter 10

1. Bob Buford, *Halftime: Changing Your Game Plan from Success to Significance* (Grand Rapids: Zondervan, 1997).

2. Eric Metaxas, *Amazing Grace: William Wilberforce and the Heroic Campaign to End Slavery* (New York: Harper One, 2007), 28.

3. Ibid., 42.

4. John Piper, *Amazing Grace in the Life of William Wilberforce* (Wheaton, Ill.: Crossway, 2006), 10.

5. Metaxas, *Amazing Grace,* 49.

6. Ibid., 133.

7. "Wilberforce and Wesley," Religion and Ethics: Christianity, http://www.bbc.co.uk/religion/religions/christianity/people/williamwilberforce_7.shtml (accessed March 21, 2008).

8. Metaxas, *Amazing Grace,* xvi.

9. Ibid., xvii.

10. Brian Kolodiejchuk, *Mother Teresa—Come Be My Light: The Private Writings of the Saint of Calcutta* (New York: Doubleday, 2007).

11. Nelson Mandela, *The Long Walk to Freedom* (New York: Little, Brown & Co., 1994).

12. Bob Buford, *Halftime: Changing Your Game Plan from Success to Significance* (Grand Rapids: Zondervan, 1997).

BOOKS BY DR. JOHN C. MAXWELL
CAN TEACH YOU HOW TO BE A REAL SUCCESS

RELATIONSHIPS

Encouragement Changes Everything

25 Ways to Win With People

Winning With People

Relationships 101

The Treasure of a Friend

The Power of Partnership in the Church

Becoming a Person of Influence

Be A People Person

The Power of Influence

Ethics 101

ATTITUDE

Success 101

The Difference Maker

How Successful People Think

The Journey From Success to Significance

Attitude 101

Failing Forward

Your Bridge to a Better Future

Living at the Next Level

The Winning Attitude

Be All You Can Be

The Power of Thinking Big

Think on These Things

The Power of Attitude

Thinking for a Change

EQUIPPING

My Dream Map

Put Your Dream to the Test

Make Today Count

The Choice Is Yours

Mentoring 101

Talent is Never Enough

Equipping 101

Developing the Leaders Around You

The 17 Essential Qualities of a Team Player

Success One Day at a Time

The 17 Indisputable Laws of Teamwork

Your Road Map for Success

Today Matters

Partners in Prayer

LEADERSHIP

Leadership Promises For Your Work Week

Leadership Gold

Go for Gold

The 21 Most Powerful Minutes
in a Leader's Day

Revised & Updated 10th Anniversary
Edition of *The 21 Irrefutable
Laws of Leadership*

The 360 Degree Leader

Leadership Promises for Every Day

Leadership 101

The Right to Lead

The 21 Indispensable Qualities of a Leader

Developing the Leader Within You

The Power of Leadership

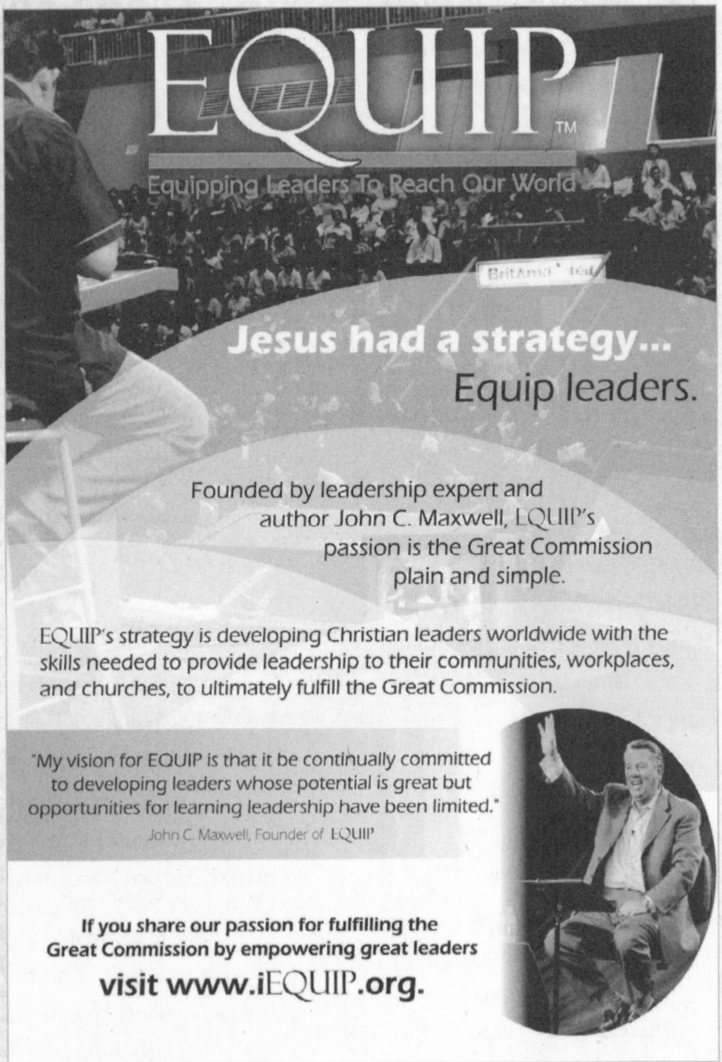
EQUIP™
Equipping Leaders To Reach Our World
Jesus had a strategy...
Equip leaders.
Founded by leadership expert and
author John C. Maxwell, EQUIP's
passion is the Great Commission
plain and simple.
EQUIP's strategy is developing Christian leaders worldwide with the skills needed to provide leadership to their communities, workplaces, and churches, to ultimately fulfill the Great Commission.
"My vision for EQUIP is that it be continually committed to developing leaders whose potential is great but opportunities for learning leadership have been limited."
John C. Maxwell, Founder of EQUIP
If you share our passion for fulfilling the Great Commission by empowering great leaders
visit www.iEQUIP.org.

$4 Billion Raised. 3,900 Churches Served.

It's an unprecedented track record. **INJOY Stewardship Services**—founded by John C. Maxwell—has partnered with over **3,900 churches** to raise over **$4 billion** for vital ministry projects. Dr. Maxwell's team of ISS consultants and specialists is helping churches to accelerate their growth and achieve their goals. **ISS** can make a lasting difference in your church, too. For more information (and some valuable resources), call ISS toll-free today at **1-800-333-6509** or visit **www.injoystewardship.com**.

"I always expected ISS to have a significant influence on churches and church leaders, but the actual impact is above and beyond all expectations. What a joy it is to see how ISS is making a difference in thousands of churches and millions of lives."

GiANT is a growth company.

We grow organizations by growing their leaders. GiANT has created many corporate training tools based on the writings of Dr. John C. Maxwell. We partner with John Maxwell to inspire transformation of self, team, and community.

LEARNING AND GROWTH EXPERIENCES

Behavior and Values Assessments

Public and Private Workshops
Leadership, Attitude, Influence, Relationships, Teamwork, Communication

Custom Corporate Training Programs
Tailored to the needs of the organization

Self Leadership Programs
Daily self-study activities to develop life-changing behaviors

Resources
Periodicals, CDs, DVDs, and more

Strategic Planning
A focused strategic thinking and execution process

Executive Coaching
Industry captains guide leaders and fast-trackers through a confidant model

Mentoring
John Maxwell's monthly Maximum Impact Club

Events
Leader retreats and exclusive conferences

MY
DREAM
MAP

An Interactive Companion to
Put Your Dream to the Test

Filled with practical applications and inspirational teaching, this companion book leads you through the process of clarifying your dream and finding the path to achieve it. *My Dream Map* also includes ample writing space for personal discovery.

LEADERSHIP.

IT ALL BEGINS WITH GOD,
THE ULTIMATE LEADER.

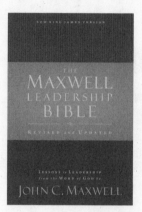

From Genesis to Revelation, the people, events, and teachings of the Bible are God's treasury of wisdom and guidance for anyone who has been called to be a person of influence. Whether you're an executive, a pastor, an entrepreneur, a parent, a coach, or a teacher, you are a leader, someone who influences and encourages others on a daily basis.

John C. Maxwell brings the laws of leadership to a new level in this revised and updated briefcase edition of *The Maxwell Leadership Bible*. Dr. Maxwell walks you through the New King James Bible text as he draws from his decades of godly leadership and best-selling resources to illuminate the time-tested and life-changing principles of leadership in Scripture. Now available in a new easy to carry size, this Bible is the ideal gift for every leader striving to be extraordinary.

FOR MORE DETAILS VISIT WWW.NELSONBIBLES.COM
OR WWW.THOMASNELSON.COM

THE GOLD STANDARD FOR LEADERS

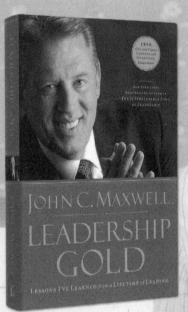